AUTISM AND FLEXISCHOOLING

by the same author

How to Make School Make Sense
A Parents' Guide to Helping the Child with Asperger Syndrome
Clare Lawrence
Foreword by Tony Attwood
ISBN 978 1 84310 664 7
eISBN 978 1 84642 834 0

Successful School Change and Transition for the Child with Asperger Syndrome
A Guide for Parents
Clare Lawrence
ISBN 978 1 84905 052 4
eISBN 978 0 85700 358 4

Asperger Syndrome – What Teachers Need to Know
Second Edition
Matt Winter
With Clare Lawrence
ISBN 978 1 84905 203 0
eISBN 978 0 85700 430 7

of related interest

Learning without School
Home Education
Ross Mountney
ISBN 978 1 84310 685 2
eISBN 978 1 84642 863 0

Teaching at Home
A New Approach to Tutoring Children with Autism and Asperger Syndrome
Olga Holland
ISBN 978 1 84310 787 3
eISBN 978 1 84642 863 0

Homeschooling the Child with Asperger Syndrome
Real Help for Parents Anywhere and On Any Budget
Lise Pyles
ISBN 978 1 84310 761 3
eISBN 978 1 84642 055 9

AUTISM AND FLEXISCHOOLING

A Shared Classroom and Homeschooling Approach

Clare Lawrence

Foreword by Dr Luke Beardon

Jessica Kingsley *Publishers*
London and Philadelphia

First published in 2012
by Jessica Kingsley Publishers
116 Pentonville Road
London N1 9JB, UK
and
400 Market Street, Suite 400
Philadelphia, PA 19106, USA

www.jkp.com

Library of Congress Cataloging in Publication Data
Lawrence, Clare.
Autism and flexischooling : a shared classroom and
homeschooling approach / Clare Lawrence ;
foreword by Luke Beardon.
p. cm.
Includes index.
ISBN 978-1-84905-279-5 (alk. paper)
1. Autistic children--Education. 2. Inclusive education. 3. Home schooling. I. Title.
LC4717.L375 2012
371.94--dc23
2012013487

British Library Cataloguing in Publication Data
A CIP catalogue record for this book is available from the British Library

ISBN 978 1 84905 279 5
eISBN 978 0 85700 582 3

Printed and bound in Great Britain

Contents

A Note on Terminology

This book uses the term 'ASD'. This is increasingly becoming an accepted term, but what does it mean? Does it include both autism and Asperger syndrome? Is Asperger syndrome the same as autism or is it something different? The initials ASD are usually taken to stand for 'autism spectrum disorder', a phrase that has been coined to incorporate both autism and Asperger syndrome, their perceived similarities and their perceived differences. However, nothing is simple and this term 'autism spectrum disorder' carries a number of difficulties.

For a start, what is this 'spectrum'? The term was first used by Lorna Wing and Judith Gould back in 1979 when it began to be understood that autism does not present as a single concrete condition but rather as something that can manifest itself over a whole spectrum of presentation. Their perception in the late seventies certainly did a great deal to widen our understanding of autism, but their term – spectrum – has been somewhat hijacked since then. Many use it to imply that there is a range of autism, and that some autism is somehow 'worse' than others. People talk about the spectrum running from 'mild' to 'severe', which misunderstands the nature of autism. Autism is a difference in the way a person's brain processes information. How can this be seen in terms of good or bad, mild or severe? Surely it is simply different?

Similarly, the term 'disorder' to stand for the the 'D' in ASD is a real problem. So much about autism has been defined in terms of 'disorder', 'disability' or 'impairment'. Perhaps this is understandable if autism is to be seen as a medical condition. Doctors do so love to find things wrong with us! Increasingly, though, autism is being understood as a difference in the way the brain works rather than as an impairment. Indeed, huge strides are being made in the 'Can Do' field of diagnosis. If someone's brain works in a different way to someone else's, surely that can be observed just as much through what that person can do better as through what he struggles with? Perhaps the difference in the way his brain processes information can be observed through superior memory or through an enhanced ability to recognise pattern or to identify musical pitch.

The debate as to whether Asperger syndrome and autism are the same condition or two different ones is further confused by the way some people have come to use the terms. Many use Asperger syndrome to describe people with autism who have average or superior intelligence. This is fine in itself, but what is far from fine is if this definition of Asperger syndrome then implies that a definition of autism must involve below average or deficient intelligence. It most certainly does not. Autism is autism, and intelligence is intelligence. Cross referencing the two is like saying that a car must be fast because it is blue. Some cars are blue and some cars are fast, but I doubt whether a driver in a Formula One race would use the colour as the deciding factor when choosing which car to race.

All of this leaves the ordinary person somewhat flummoxed. The people this book is written for – parents and teachers and children with an ASD – are unlikely to be too concerned with the ebb and flow of the autism vs Asperger vs spectrum debate. They merely want to get on with it. So, throughout this book I have used the term ASD as shorthand. It stands, for me, for an autism spectrum difference: 'autism' because that is the proper name for this different way of neuro-processing; 'spectrum' because that is the current most accepted way to include Asperger syndrome and 'difference' because that is what it is. Autism is a difference and as Gunilla Gerland, a woman with autism wrote, being different is just as good as being like everyone else (Gerland in Hesmondhalgh and Breakey, 2001, p.45).

Foreword

The clue is in the title – specifically, the word 'flexi'. Representative of 'flexible' when used in compound words, is one of the critical concepts that can lead to successful lives for people with autism. Individuals with autism are well known for being rather rigid and inflexible; ironically, however, many individuals and parents actually find that the rigidity of 'the system' (in this instance, educational institutions and the wider education agenda) is what is holding their child back or, in many cases, actually harming their child. The lack of flexibility in teaching styles, teaching environments, temporality (i.e. duration of lessons), the sensory environment and curriculum – to cite just a few – can cause extreme problems for the child with autism. What Clare identifies is an exceptionally effective potential solution to many, if not all, of the problems faced by parent, teacher and child.

Clare writes with enviable clarity and intelligence. She makes very good sense in an area that traditionally is highly complex. Her arguments are sound and many of what she highlights as problematic areas in critical need of change will resonate with so many parents of children with autism. Educational years are crucial to the development of the child; equally, if the child is exposed to difficult situations in those years the impact can be huge. Seemingly inconsequential events can lead to major problems later in life; the day-to-day grind of being exposed to an often bewildering, chaotic, stressful and demanding mainstream school for the autistic individual can have a massive and devastating impact on self-esteem, confidence and mental health. It is vital that all options are explored in order to reduce the very real risk to the individual.

I absolutely agree with the underpinning concept that changes in the environment are required to enable the child to reach potential, rather than trying ineffectually to change the child. The greater the range of options that are available to parents of children with autism, the better. Flexischooling is absolutely not the best option for *all* children with autism – clearly the heterogeneity of the population is such that any such generalisation would be a crass, misleading suggestion; however, it is equally as clear that for some children with autism, flexischooling is an option that could be the answer to an otherwise devastating situation. Clare's book on flexischooling is an excellent introduction to how it can be of benefit to the child with autism; any parent of an autistic child, plus anyone with an interest in the education of children with autism should read this book.

Dr Luke Beardon
Senior Lecturer in Autism at The Autism
Centre, Sheffield Hallam University

Introduction

Why Would We
Want to Do That?

Mainstream inclusion:
where are we now?

This book considers 'flexischooling' as a way to support the child with an autism spectrum difference (ASD) into mainstream school. Perhaps implied in this is a suspicion that sending children with an ASD into full-time mainstream school, under the 'Inclusion' philosophy in place in education at the moment, may not always work for all of those children, all of the time.

Inclusion of children with Special Educational Needs involves enabling them to access their education through attending mainstream school alongside their peers. It involves adapting these schools, and that education, to provide the support necessary for the children to experience the same range of facilities and opportunities as their peers. This Inclusion model has largely replaced the old Segregation model, and now children with all but the most complex and severe Special Educational Needs are educated in mainstream schools rather than in special schools. The argument is that all children, as far as is possible, deserve the same access to education and opportunities, and no one, I think, is arguing against that basic philosophy.

The debate, however, is about how well Inclusion is meeting the needs of all children. It is a debate largely beyond the scope of this book (it is very well explored in the fascinating set of essays, *Included or Excluded*, edited by Ruth Cigman, 2007). The question under discussion is how well this system is meeting the needs of children with Special Educational Needs, and particularly some children with an ASD. Both Mary Warnock, who wrote the original 1978 report that advocated Inclusion, and Lorna Wing, one of the foremost experts on ASDs, agree that in some ways Inclusion is not always working for children with an ASD. They argue that, for some children with an ASD, their needs would be more fully met by an option of specialist provision – by smaller class sizes, more expert teaching and a quieter and more ordered environment. They argue the case that, while Inclusion should always be an option open to all children, for some this actually amounts to a 'painful kind of exclusion' (Warnock in Cigman, 2007).

Whether specialist provision for children with an ASD will become more widely available in the future, or will be seen as more desirable, remains to be seen. What is certain, at the moment, is that it is not an option that is available to very many. Given the closure of many special schools, for most children with an ASD and particularly those with 'high functioning' autism or Asperger syndrome, mainstream remains the only school option and it is for these children and their families that this book is written.

If experts agree that these children may require more specialist support than most mainstream schools can offer, and that many aspects of the mainstream environment remain unsuited to the needs of a child with an ASD however hard the staff at that school try to adapt them, what alternatives can the parents of a child with an ASD consider? If, for some children, 'involuntary inclusion is as problematic as involuntary segregation' (Sinclair in Cigman, 2007), what can you, as a parent in the real world of today, do to help your child with an ASD?

Why consider flexischooling?

Many children with an ASD and Asperger syndrome will manage mainstream school well. There is some excellent support available and very often dedicated staff can make this challenging environment both more accessible and more comprehensible for the pupil with an ASD.

However, sometimes things go wrong. If you, like me, are a parent of a child with an ASD, you are likely to know this already. You will know that in spite of everyone's best efforts, for some children with an ASD school is a confusing, hostile, frightening and horrible place. For these children and their parents, and indeed for the staff who try hard to make things work but who realise that they are failing, the situation becomes something of a nightmare.

You may recognise the scenario: every morning you have to prise your child's fingers off the doorpost just to get him into the car. The school contacts you on a near daily basis to report that he has lashed out, had to be removed from class, has run away. Other parents report tales from their children of screaming and uproar in the classroom. Your child is being singled out as different, is teased and even bullied. Even on 'good days' when there are no specific incidents you know that he is just shutting down and is learning nothing. He is socially isolated and has made no friends. His behaviour at home is becoming increasingly worrying. He is biting on his arm, banging his head on the walls. His temper flares out of control. He is becoming more and more difficult to reach and you feel you are losing him. You barely manage to steer him safely through the evenings and weekends and are beginning to dread the holidays. Your other children are fed up and your partner is threatening to leave home. No one ever seems to have the time to get together to sort out a way forward. You are all unhappy, your child most of all. What can anyone do to help?

This nightmare scenario is not really as rare as it feels when you are going through it in isolation. It is an experience familiar to many parents of children with an ASD of many ages and in many countries. If this is your situation, flexischooling just may offer an answer – for you, for the school and for your child. It is an option that is not explored as often as perhaps it should be, and it is one that may well be worth considering.

This book will guide you through why flexischooling might work for your child with an ASD. Incidentally, for ease, I will usually refer to the child with an ASD as 'he', but that in no way implies that girls with autism and Asperger syndrome are any less in need, nor that flexischooling isn't just as good an option for them. It is…but using 'he' makes the grammar easier! For either your son or daughter with an ASD, I hope this book will help you decide whether to give flexischooling a try and will answer some of your questions and address some of your doubts about it.

Let's be very clear, though: this is your choice. No one should ever put any pressure on you to suggest that your child attends school part time if it is not what you want. Your child is entitled to a full-time place in school. If you and the school decide between you to try out an option where some of that full-time education takes place at home, that is your decision and the school's. Flexischooling can be a great option for the child with an ASD, but it should be in addition to, not instead of, the other support offered to your child that the school has a responsibility to put into place.

What is flexischooling?

Flexischooling is when a child attends school for part of the time and is educated at home for the remainder of the time. It is just one term used for this: 'Part-Time School Attendance', 'Flexi-Time Attendance', 'Partial Homeschooling', 'Partial Independent Study Program' are all other terms. It has been defined as: 'The part-time arrangement whereby school and family share responsibility for the child's education in an agreed contract and partnership' (Meighan in Oliver, 2000). There are many different ways to set it up and it describes a whole range of different provision. However, the important point is that it describes a shared responsibility and partnership and it is this that may make it so suitable for the child with an ASD.

Can anyone do it?

Yes. You need no special qualifications and do not need to be a teacher nor an ASD expert. What you do need is time and energy and enough belief in both yourself and in your child to give it a go. How common it is as an option will vary according to where you live. In California, up to 10 per cent of students on a school's register may be enrolled at least part of the time in an Independent Study Program whereas in the UK only a very few families may have even heard of flexischooling. If it seems an unusual option for some of you, take heart – it can work, so don't let that stop you!

Is it legal?

Clearly, different countries have different laws and it would be impossible to go into full legal details in a book such as this, but the answer, of course, is 'yes!' It is your responsibility, as a parent, to ensure that your child receives a suitable, full-time education. Most parents choose to do this by sending their child to school full time, and some do so by teaching their child full time at home. Some, as here, work with a school so that together they can share delivery of the best possible education for that child. That is the key: the child's education must be full time and it must be suitable to the needs of that child. In the perfect flexischooling model for the pupil with an ASD the consistency across environments, the time to explain, reassure and unpick problems, the improved social engagement with parents, the opportunities for 1:1 teaching and for supported independent learning, the respect for the needs of the child's ASD and the opportunities for him to understand and appreciate his own condition all make a thoroughly effective, full-time education that entirely fulfils the requirements of the law.

Is it a right?

No, although you do have the right to request it and for that request to be considered seriously on its own merits. What you are asking in the flexischooling model is that you be given the opportunity to share the responsibility for your child's education with the school. This is a reasonable request and schools must consider it. In England, the Badman report (Badman, 2009) recommended that schools 'extend and make available the opportunities of flexi-schooling', and most schools are now aware that they have an obligation to consider these requests and, indeed, to agree to them unless they have reason to refuse. On the other hand, their reason to refuse may simply be that they cannot see any way that it can be made to work as the best option for either school or child.

Your job is to explain how and why it works (which is what this book is all about!), and to persuade the school that you can work with it for the good of all. If the school agrees to this way of working, you need to be aware that in many ways this is a privilege and not a right, and work courteously with the school. Flexischooling can, most certainly, work brilliantly, but it takes co-operation and teamwork, right from the start.

Can I change my mind?

Yes. If you try flexischooling and either you, your child or the school do not feel that it is working, your child will still have his full-time place at the school and will still be entitled to the support in school that he would have had before. In this sense there is no issue of 'burning your bridges'. This can make flexischooling a less drastic option to try than, say, full-time homeschooling where you withdraw your child from the system and risk losing your child his place at that school.

Is it part-time education?

No. This is an essential point. A child's education has to be full time, and there is nothing part time about flexischooling, just about school attendance. What you are doing by setting up a flexischooling arrangement is agreeing that school is not the only, nor always the best, place for your child with an ASD to learn. The rest of his education will happen outside school, and you will be responsible for that time. This will include actual lesson work (history, English, science and so on) but need not only be academic learning: many 'real-life' skills that a person with an ASD is going to have to master – independent travel, managing money, shopping, organising his day, cooking and cleaning and other independent living skills – can be best practised in an out-of-school context too.

Is it more suited to the child with lower academic potential?

Not at all. One of the problems with school is that the individual with an ASD may well be underachieving and may not reach the level of which he is capable. Just managing in school may be taking up most of his energy. School is a busy and social environment. Working out what to do, what to say, how to behave, how to avoid the unkindness – both intentional and unintentional – of others, all may be taking up most of his concentration, leaving little left for academic learning. Add to this the environmental stresses of lights, movement, smells, sudden bells and announcement systems and you have a place where learning is likely to be very difficult indeed.

Many children with an ASD have considerable intellectual abilities, and if their learning needs can be understood and met and if they are supported to manage these needs, they can fulfil this potential to the highest standards. ASDs occur across the whole intellectual range and many people, often diagnosed with Asperger syndrome or high functioning autism, are very bright indeed. Some of the world's greatest thinkers and achievers have conditions on the autistic spectrum; how many more people are out there with just such gifts but who have been unable to fulfil their potential because their learning needs were not fully understood?

Isn't it the school's responsibility to meet his needs?

The flexischooling approach described in this book explores a working relationship between home and school.

Most schools will work very hard to meet the needs of children with an ASD, and many of their strategies are very successful. What is suggested here is not designed to negate the work they are doing nor to undermine their skills and expertise. Rather, it seeks to recognise that since ASDs bring a unique set of challenges, and since school by its very nature is a socially orientated environment, one way to help the pupil with an ASD is to share his education between home and school. This book gives many examples of how and why flexischooling works so well for the pupil with an ASD, but it is most unlikely to work at all if parents and school cannot act as a team. What the parents do at home should support, explain, enhance and develop what is done in school. If you, as a parent, feel that you cannot work with your child's school then this may not be the best path to consider. Nor is it a path you should feel that you have to consider if you do not feel it is suitable to you or your situation. Yes – schools have a responsibility to meet the needs of your child, and working with the school to meet those needs full time always remains an option. Flexischooling is only one way forward and you should never feel pushed into it unless it is something you really want to try.

If school is so inappropriate, why not just home educate?

Some parents of children with an ASD do take this option, and for many of them it works very well. For further information on this, the book *Home Educating our Autistic Spectrum Children: Paths are Made by Walking* (Dowty and Cowlishaw, 2001) is a great place to start. Flexischooling is not designed to replace full-time homeschooling as an option, merely to offer a further alternative. There may be some aspects of full-time homeschooling that can make it difficult for some parents, and for them flexischooling can offer a further choice.

What flexischooling allows is a way for some home education to be a more accessible option for some parents, and simultaneously to allow school to be more appropriate. Rather than an 'either/or' scenario, flexischooling may provide a way to allow the pupil with an ASD 'the best of both worlds'.

So, why does it work so well?

Part 1

A CONSIDERATION OF FLEXISCHOOLING

Chapter 1

Why Does Flexischooling Work so Well for the Pupil with an ASD?

Before we look at this question, let's see why school itself is such a challenge for the pupil with an ASD.

For a start, it may be important to say that I am not 'anti school'. I am, in fact, a teacher and I understand schools and appreciate how hard the professionals involved in them work. I believe that most teachers do a wonderful job and that there have been terrific strides made over the last ten years or so to better understand and meet the needs of children with an ASD. Supported by dedicated and increasingly experienced Special Educational Needs Co-ordinators (SENCOs), teaching aides and learning-support assistants, teachers are doing a great deal to make school a more welcoming environment for children with an ASD. I have written a number of books suggesting ways that schools can be helped to 'make sense' for the pupil with an ASD, and I firmly believe that this can and should be done.

On the other hand, it is always going to be something of an uphill struggle. So much of what school actually is makes it a very challenging place for the child with an ASD. Schools are noisy, busy places. Children are taught in groups, and thinking in schools tends to be around groups, not around the individual. This is understandable: the system allows for only one or possibly two adults in a classroom of perhaps 30 or more children. The 30 need to be dealt with together if the system is going to work. There is little leeway for the one child who does not join the group, who needs to go off by himself, wants to read when the others are singing, or needs to repeat out loud when the others are working quietly. A great deal of work on including the child with an ASD into the school is on finding ways of getting him to join the group. Will he come and sit at circle time if he has his own mat to sit on? Can he join the line if he is allowed to stand at the back? Will he be able to manage singing practice if he can wear headphones? Can he cope with lunch break if he brings an item connected with his special interest with him to distract him from all those people milling around?

These are all good strategies and many will work, but the question must remain to be asked: is all this work on persuading a child to join the group really going to make much difference when, by diagnosis, he is not a group player? All of these strategies are designed to desensitise to stress, or to find ways to make the confusing more comprehensible, and there is a place for this in the education of a child with an ASD. The 'real world' does involve many of these situations…but never again to quite the same degree. How many adults sit cross-legged in a massed group singing, unless they choose to do so?

On the other hand, school does give an opportunity for the person with an ASD to try out these situations with some support to hand. One of the disadvantages of full-time homeschooling for the child with an ASD is that group situations such as these can be totally avoided, and so the opportunity for developing strategies to cope with them may be missed. Many adults with an ASD have their options in life severely restricted because they feel they cannot manage crowds or noise or being trapped in a group situation. What school can do – at its best – is to provide these opportunities but with a 'safety net', so that individuals can develop strategies that work for them and so have access to a full range of activities and situations into the future.

It is also undoubtedly true that the decision to take your child completely out of school and home educate him full time is not one to be taken lightly. It involves a massive commitment of time and energy, and you will be working largely on your own. True, there is a growing number of home education groups but since the reasons to home educate are as many and as varied as the people themselves, it may be that support around your child and your issues may be hard to find. As far as 'mainstream' support goes, by choosing to home educate you may be largely cutting yourself off. This can be a lonely experience and such a step may be more than many parents are prepared to take.

Perhaps one of the hidden advantages of flexischooling over full-time homeschooling is that the child with an ASD, who then becomes an adult with an ASD, will still accumulate some of the shared experiences that are the currency of growing up. 'Where did you go to school?', 'Didn't you just hate geography?', 'Who was your favourite teacher?'; so many of us assume the common childhood experience of going to school. Without this experience, the person with an ASD, who may feel distanced from society and from other individuals already because of his condition, may find himself even further adrift. If you don't go to school, you miss that shared experience. If you do go to school, whether that is all the time or just for three mornings a week, you retain your understanding of what so many other people are going on about!

So why else is flexischooling an option so worth considering for the pupil with an ASD? Is it simply that it still is school, but not for so long? Is it because it has the advantages of a home education, but again without the full-time intensity? It combines the advantages of a shorter time at school (but still some time) with a longer time at home (but not all), and may just result in something that truly is the best of all worlds.

A shorter time in school

At its most fundamental, this is the great strength of flexischooling. School becomes a less intense issue simply because there is 'less of it'. The total immersion nature of the usual school experience is lessened, and the whole experience becomes less all-consuming. Many issues that would usually cause flare-ups and distress can be managed, because much of the intensity has been taken out of the situation.

The child is less exhausted socially

Your child is likely to find the challenge of decoding social expectations, constantly interacting socially and generally 'fitting in' with the rest of his peers exhausting. What comes pretty naturally to the neurotypical (or non-autistic) child is a tremendous challenge to the child with an ASD. In order to manage socially he is going to have to use a great deal of conscious effort, and will not be able to rely on subconscious instinct in the same way another child might do. Working out what others mean, what he is expected to do and say, what is implied and what he should infer – all these take enormous effort. Social success depends on getting these things right. The child who is in school part time has a greater chance of being able to focus – hard – on these things for the shorter time, and, by getting them right, of achieving a higher level of social acceptance.

He can concentrate on subjects enjoyed and be a success

Perhaps your child is good at, and interested in, science. Perhaps he is a natural musician or a talented artist. Perhaps he enjoys solving mathematical puzzles. All of us tend to enjoy what we are good at, and flexischooling allows the pupil to pick and choose subjects he is better at, or with which he is more comfortable. Even if he does not show a particular flair for a subject, there will be some things that suit him better than others. As a general rule (although by no means always), children with an ASD struggle with sports options, especially those involving team games. Many children with an ASD are physically uncoordinated and this, together with difficulty 'reading' the social cues of a team game, can make sports very difficult. Others may dread drama, with its element of 'let's pretend' and unreality or find a foreign language difficult when they already struggle to find the right words even in their own tongue.

Flexischooling allows a tailoring of the at-school curriculum to better suit your child. This does not mean that he should never try the subjects or areas he finds difficult, but, it does mean that there can be some sensitivity around exposing him to too much challenge, too much of the time. More challenging subjects can be introduced gently, during his 1:1 home time. Meanwhile, by allowing him to concentrate his efforts at school around where he is most likely to succeed, it is possible to 'weigh the dice' a little in his favour and help him on the road to success.

Potential problems are averted and flare-ups avoided

This 'weighing the dice' means that the child with an ASD need not be exposed to experiences that he simply cannot handle. Sometimes these will be individual experiences (attending crowded assemblies, for instance, or joining in with whole-group singing or music-making) and sometimes they will be cumulative. A pupil might enjoy the first part of the day, and manage to 'hold it together' during morning break, but by midday might simply be overwhelmed and exhausted. This is the point at which he may snap and put himself into a situation which is simply unacceptable. The child who resorts to hitting or spitting, lashing out or running away may quite simply have run out of other options to express his distress. Incidents like this have a long-lasting negative effect – on the teachers who are on the receiving end, the pupils who are involved, other staff and parents and most of all the pupil himself. It is far better to find a way to give him an 'out' before it gets this bad. If he knows that he will be out of school in just an hour's time he may well be able to 'hold it together' for that time until he is able to self-repair at home.

Misunderstandings can be unpicked and repaired

Sometimes, problems will still occur. If everything that is said and done needs to be consciously scrutinised and interpreted it is not surprising if sometimes the pupil will make mistakes. These may be relatively simple (mistaking a room or a teacher, for example) or more complex (such as misunderstanding a series of instructions so that his behaviour is inappropriate or he appears defiant). Very often a pupil with an ASD may appear unwilling to comply simply because of misinterpretation. If, for example, he has been asked to go to Mr Black's room and is found in Miss White's room, the natural response may be to give a penal mark or whatever sanction the school uses. However, what is needed is the time to dig down to find out *why* he is in the wrong room. Does he know where Mr Black's room is? Do both parties mean the same thing by 'Mr Black's room'? (Is he, in fact, looking for the room where he last saw Mr Black when the teacher meant the room where Mr Black is now?) Has another member of staff given him conflicting instructions since, perhaps found him in the corridor and told him to get to his English lesson without waiting to find out where he is heading in the first place?

Sorting out even simple problems like these takes time, and time can be a scarce commodity in the busy life of the school day. The neurotypical, non-autistic child will usually be vociferous in pointing out unfairness, but the child with an ASD may lack the communication skills to make his case clearly or calmly, and the 'unfairness' of what is happening may well overwhelm him. With flexischooling comes time to sort out problems, as they occur. If your child is only in school for the morning session it is possible to find out if any incidents have occurred during that time and try to get to the bottom of misunderstandings straight away. If he is in school all day the incidents of the morning are likely to have been submerged by the incidents of lunchtime and the afternoon and before anyone knows it the child is mired in confusion and resentment.

Behaviour can be more 'normal' leading to greater social acceptance

If your child has to cope with the challenges of the whole day by himself he will have to self-repair in any way he can. Unfortunately, the way that a person with an ASD looks after himself can be exactly the reason that he gets into difficulties. Perhaps he hand-flaps or sucks on his sleeve; perhaps he monologues about his special interest; perhaps he seeks solitude to go into his inner world but by doing so leaves himself open to being targeted by those Professor Tony Attwood (2007, Chapter 4) calls 'the predators'. The very things that the person with an ASD does to relieve the pressure of coping in the socially demanding world of school are the things that lay him open to social ridicule, rejection and danger.

The person with an ASD should never have to pretend to be 'normal': there is *nothing* to be ashamed about in having an ASD! His ways of coping and managing his condition, if they work for him, are valid and to be respected. He should be allowed to do as he wants, to pursue his own interests and pleasures, as long as they do not infringe anyone else's rights. However, in society in general, and in the society of school in particular, to do something different from the norm is to be 'odd'. Social acceptance relies on fitting in and being seen to be the same as everyone else.

The ideal is that he manages to behave in a 'socially acceptable' (i.e. neurotypical) way for the time he is in school because he knows he will have access to his ASD behaviour, if he wishes, when he comes out. As soon as he is back at home he may go off into his inner world, may drive you insane by talking on and on about spaceship sightings or perform all manner of complex body movements or rituals. All are fine – they are his way of coping. They will be serving a purpose, for him, and as such should not be stopped. It is just safer and more acceptable if he can learn the trick of not doing these things at school.

Bullying can be addressed and avoided

Bullying is a serious issue for the child with an ASD. Most schools will tell you that they have a policy to deal with it – that they have it under control – yet so many adults with an ASD report terrible misery during their school years because of the words and actions of their peers. Pupils with an ASD, particularly those at mainstream school, are at increased risk of being bullied (Little in Attwood, 2008). Fifty-nine per cent of parents of children with 'high functioning' autism or Asperger syndrome in a National Autistic Society (NAS) survey said that their child had been bullied (Batten *et al.*, 2006). As well as name-calling, ostracising and excluding, physical taunts and ridicule, the child with an ASD is vulnerable to being 'set up' to do things that get him into trouble. His social naivety makes him a target, as do his different behaviours and his social isolation.

There is work that can be done around the issue of a pupil with an ASD being bullied and all schools will, also, have a general policy on preventing bullying. These can be very successful, but they take considerable commitment and time. In the meantime, flexischooling offers a practical and more or less instant solution.

There will be 'areas' where the bullying occurs – both geographical areas and areas of the school day. Usually the most dangerous times are unstructured and unsupervised times such as breaks and lunchtimes, the lavatories and when getting changed for sports. There may also be some lessons where bullying has occurred and not been controlled, and where it may then reoccur. Some teachers, sadly, are not in full control of all pupils at all times. When this happens, they themselves are likely to be subjected to bullying (watching a pack of adolescents turning on a single teacher can be a frightening and eye-opening experience), and there is little safety to be had for your child from this adult. Your child probably relies on adult rules to make sense of the world of school and so may find this situation particularly alarming and distressing.

If he is flexischooling he has the one magic option not open to the other children (nor to the teacher!): he can avoid that class in future. Similarly, it is usually possible to structure the in-school time for the flexischooled child to avoid the danger areas, whether these are lunchtimes, games lessons or whatever. Simply by not being there, he can avoid a great deal of unpleasantness.

There is also, though, a more covert advantage. By flexischooling he is already acknowledging his difference and this itself may defuse a great deal of the need for others to taunt. There is little satisfaction in pointing out that someone is 'weird', 'odd' or 'different' if it is an accepted fact, and peer groups seem to find this less socially acceptable. It seems that the great crime as seen by the adolescent pack is to pretend to belong when you don't. If you acknowledge that you don't, and particularly if you are confident in yourself, including in your difference, your presence is often far more acceptable and it may even be that you are accepted into the pack on these new terms. The sociology of the pack instincts of the young is a complex subject but it seems to be the case that the young person who happily and confidently acknowledges that he is different, who in addition is not trapped in the situation without escape and is therefore not fearful or distressed, may well be less likely to be targeted as a victim.

Parents, school and pupil working together makes for shared responsibility and understanding

In a way, perhaps, this is the greatest strength of all. The problem with the usual school experience is that it is just so enormously busy. There is little time written into the system to allow you to explain your child's behaviour, or for you to find out what does work for your child in school. There is little time for the health professionals working with your child to explain interventions either to you or to the school, and very little hope if they explain to one that their information will arrive clearly with the other. Teachers and support staff go on training and put into place a whole wealth of interventions, but they don't usually have much time or opportunity to explain these to you as parents, so you are seldom able to continue the same supports at home. Rather than consistency and sameness over all environments, the child with an ASD is left to adapt to the different styles and approaches of the different parts of his life.

Worse, there may begin to be a culture of blame between the different environments. I have heard many parents say that the school will not listen to them and does not really understand their child's needs. Similarly, I have heard teachers and other professionals in school bewailing the fact that the structure and order put into place at school is not carried on at home. Health professionals regret that they cannot get into school often enough to observe and suggest strategies. The result is that three of the most important elements in the child's life are not working together. The fourth element, the child himself, may be lost as each tries to show that their way is best.

Clearly this is far from ideal, but it is understandable. Schools are very busy places. There is little or no spare time available during busy days to make time to explain to parents or even entertain too much intervention from health professionals. Health professionals too have busy schedules, and parents have their own lives. In the normal course of events, parents send their children off to school secure that they are safe and learning, and in doing so give themselves the opportunity to work themselves. The system is simply not set up for there to be too much overlap between the different worlds.

Flexischooling alters this. By setting up a shared experience of educating the child, the school and parents

– and often health professionals too – have to work together. By definition this is a shared responsibility. Ways to solve problems and to get around difficulties can be handed on, strategies and techniques can be used consistently. Above all, communication can take place and all the parties can begin to work together to come up with a unique, tailor-made strategy that will work best for that child at that time. Together, everyone can make it work.

A longer time at home

If flexischooling works because it takes the heat out of the full-time nature of school, nevertheless there is more to the home-time element than just being 'not school'. Your child's education must be full time, and if attendance at school is only part time, the remainder of that education is going to have to take place at home. This is both a daunting responsibility and a tremendous opportunity.

ASDs cannot – at least currently – be diagnosed through blood tests or antenatal scans, nor are they apparent in a baby at birth. One of the traumas for the parents of a child with an ASD is that they have to come to terms with the fact that their child is 'not who they thought he was', as they face up to the truth of the diagnosis. Many parents will not have come to terms with this diagnosis by the time their child starts school and indeed some may not even be aware that their child has an ASD at this time.

Yet there is intense pressure to get an early diagnosis when an ASD is suspected, in order not to 'miss the early window' of child development. Some researchers imply that early intervention is vital in order to achieve the best outcome into adult life, and the anxious parent may be bombarded by sometimes-conflicting advice, always with one eye on the clock and an awareness that time is ticking by.

This sense of panic and urgency can be distressing and can add further to the pressure already felt by many parents. At least some of this comes from the knowledge that the parents' time with the child is limited as the prospect of school looms. Many parents are left feeling that once their child enters the school system they have missed their only opportunity to reach out to their child and somehow combat the 'monster' that – they may believe at that time – is autism.

It is, after all, unlikely at this stage that the parent will know very much about ASDs. As such, they may, indeed, view ASDs as outside agents 'attacking' their child, and feel that something to be overcome or subdued. Understanding and acceptance and even, ultimately, real appreciation take time and, although many parents become highly knowledgeable and expert about their child's condition, and indeed well able to celebrate the good in it, this does not happen overnight. At the point of a child's diagnosis, his parents are unlikely to know any more about ASDs than anyone else in the general population. They may suffer from the same ignorance and misconception and, additionally, are likely to be feeling vulnerable, distressed and angry. What they need is shared provision and shared expertise, time and support and they are ill-served by the 'too late, too late!' rhetoric of those who rush the care of their children into school and out of their hands.

Flexischooling removes much of the panic of urgency about the artificial barrier of school age. When your child goes into school, this need no longer be the end of your intense involvement. Simultaneously, flexischooling allows you, as a parent, access to expertise as it is available in schools. School and parent working together can provide the knowledge, the commitment, the care and the time needed to give your child the best education, right through to adulthood.

Of course, education does not stop there, nor for very many parents of a child with an ASD does their intense parental responsibility. Over 40 per cent of adults with autism live with their parents, and over 60 per cent rely on family for their financial support (Rosenblatt, 2008). Since so many parents are in this for the long haul, their knowledge, skill, understanding and involvement need to be supported and developed, right from the start. Schools can help do this, and the teamwork involved in flexischooling, particularly when it also involves other ASD and healthcare experts, can provide a framework within which the child with an ASD can grow to adulthood with the best possible chance of confidence and success.

Missing skills can be targeted as shopping, travelling, etc. will be quieter during practice hours

A child with an ASD is likely to be very uneven in his development. Perhaps he can tell you every make, number and size of bus used on the London network, but he may be unable to tell you the months of the year in order. He may have memorised the periodic table of elements but have little concept of money, be unable to tell the time, and not be reliably continent even into teenage years. He may struggle with all sorts of skills from asking questions to making choices, from queuing to crossing the road.

If he is flexischooling this gives a golden opportunity to spend more time on essential skills. During the evening and weekends everywhere is busy. During mainstream schooling, a certain level of maturity and skill will be taken for granted. If the child with an ASD needs extra practice in crossing the road safely, for example, extra provision needs to be made and this may not always be easy to arrange in a mainstream setting.

The great thing about flexischooling is that it gives you an opportunity to practise skills with him when shops, roads, stations, etc. are less busy, and – even more importantly – it gives you dedicated time in which to do it. Flexischooling time is when your other children are at school, your partner is at work and you have this time designated as 1:1 time to spend with your child. Without flexischooling you may be left trying to give support with these missing skills when also dealing with other children, the family shop and a mobile phone call from a colleague at work. This is hardly easy. Giving yourself specific, dedicated time to spend with your child with an ASD may be just what you need to create real and much-needed opportunities.

Interests and skills can be developed

Conversely, as well as missing many skills the neurotypical person takes for granted, the person with an ASD may have a number of interests and talents that should be nurtured. Flexischooling gives time to focus on these and to allow them to develop. As home study time can be truly child centred, this learning can follow the child's lead. Whether a passion for investigating bug types, a talent for playing the trumpet or expertise in identifying different brands of chocolate by taste, the child's individual interests and skills are important and well worth nurturing. These interests or skills may seem odd or insignificant now, but they may grow and develop into life-long passions and expertise, leading to otherwise undreamed-of educational and professional possibilities. Even more important, they probably give him a huge amount of joy!

Through home study time the child will be given a far greater than usual opportunity to develop self-directed study. The child with an ASD is unlikely to be someone who learns well from the group experience. He is, however, likely to be someone who learns extremely well from the individual experience. Asocial learning– learning which takes place out of a social context – is something that can be difficult to organise in a school setting. How do you keep track of 30 or more children all learning their own thing in their own way? It is much easier for the teacher to direct the group to learn together, so that she can keep track of what they are supposed to achieve and who does or does not manage this. At home, though, the child with an ASD can manage his own learning and his own way of learning.

The internet has revolutionised how we all access information. Twenty years ago, the child trying to learn away from school may well have been handicapped by lack of resources. This is no longer the case. There are myriad learning resources for all levels, ages and abilities, available online. The child who wants to learn by himself has, now, every opportunity to do so.

The great thing about the home-study element of the flexischooled child's school day is how the skills of self-motivated learning and self-directed study will stand him in good stead into the future. As an adult, these skills and this way of working can lead seamlessly to any number and level of qualifications, and indeed to employment. It could even be argued that the child who spends some of his school day learning independently at home is preparing himself far more suitably for the world of work in the 21st century than the child who spends all of his day in a school environment. After all, working from home is no longer seen as eccentric. Why should schooling from home be seen any differently?

Motivation can be specific, making less appealing subjects approachable

One of the biggest frustrations of trying to teach a child with an ASD is his ability to switch off and to mentally 'go somewhere else' if he is not interested! One child described this as 'like having a laptop computer in my head that always has an internet connection to my memory' (Lawrence, 2008), and it is hardly surprising if, with this available, the child chooses to use it when what is being taught in the real world is difficult or dull. A child with an ASD may not be motivated by praise or reward in quite the same way as his neurotypical peers. A sticker or a 'Well Done!' stamp may not be enough to bring him back to struggling with multiplication problems if his other, far more fascinating, world beckons.

A parent working 1:1 with the child at home is far better placed than the school to offer immediate motivation and reward. With no other 30 or more children to take into account, the parent can offer whatever works in exchange for the attention required. Ten correct multiplication answers may be worth an immediate ten minutes on a computer game or ten minutes playing with the current special interest toy, the opportunity to tell ten interesting facts or even ten chocolate buttons. All work, and all motivation, can be immediate, appropriate and accessible to the child, and this can help learning enormously.

The special interest can be used

Linked to motivation (above) is the child's special interest. Many children with an ASD have an overwhelming and absorbing passion for one particular subject. What this subject is may change over time, but the intensity of interest will probably just switch to something new. People with an ASD can have astonishing focus and concentration when dealing with this subject of interest. For the teacher in a school context it really is most unlikely that she will be able to get and keep the child's interest in 'The Use of the Capital Letter' when all the child really cares about is the relative speeds of asteroids.

The great joy of 1:1 teaching and learning at home is that it can go with, rather than fight against, the special interest. The child with an ASD needs to be learning, and perhaps as important, learning to learn. So much of this can happen naturally as you support him to find out more about what interests him. He desperately wants to learn more about asteroids: take him to the library and find him books, take him to talks at the local astronomy society, help him use the marvellous resources of the internet, help him find online groups, calculate where the next asteroid storm will be sighted, investigate environmental, geographical and meteorological factors that influence good sightings...the possibilities are endless. The great joys are that at no time are you imposing learning on your child, you are probably learning a great deal yourself(!) and, perhaps best of all, you are sharing an interest with your child. He may not be keen to let you in (you are not going to 'solve' the autism barrier overnight), but you have more chance of making contact with him through sharing his interest than trying to force your interests on him.

The child with an ASD can 'self-repair'

Equally, as mentioned above, the child with an ASD should be allowed, indeed encouraged, to use his own methods of self-calming. Although many people in the neurotypical world may seek to stop these 'autistic-like' behaviours (flapping, monologuing, talking or singing to himself, burrowing under cushions, spinning or other repetitive or ritualised movements), if they work for the individual they must be valid. Equally, simply being by himself may be all the person with an ASD needs to recharge and be able to face the socially orientated world once again. Most parents of a child with an ASD will recognise the frustration of their child coming home from school in a foul mood, answering questions about school in monosyllables and slamming up to his bedroom for the evening alone. Such parents often feel helpless and useless and, even though they are aware that their child is unhappy and probably 'failing' at school, do not know how to find a way in to help. For them, allowing time in the school day for their child to recover and recharge, can free up other time where interaction is more possible and they can find ways to connect with and support their child better.

Formal 1:1 study time can provide a way in for parents
Connecting with a child with an ASD can be daunting. Many parents feel shut out by their child, right from the early days when as a baby he cried when held or as a toddler he wriggled out of a hug. Many parents of children with an ASD have found that their child does not bring things to show them, does not ask questions about the world or even ask for treats. Their child may not run to them when hurt, cling to them at parting nor express any pleasure when reunited. Parenting a child with an ASD is tough just because the 'normal' links of need and love are not there, or at least not obvious.

For these parents, a greater involvement in their child's education can be a tremendous boost. At age four, when the typical child begins to spend most of his day at school, the child with an ASD may not yet have made any real connection with his parents. If this child is then 'handed over' to the education system in the usual way, further opportunities may be scarce. After school hours and at weekends there may be other children to consider, all of whom are likely to be more demanding in their neurotypical way than the child with an ASD. There is work to be done – the usual jobs and shopping, washing and living – and there may not be the time nor space to set up interaction opportunities with a child who seems to reject these approaches. If the parent feels a failure already, there is even less likelihood that he or she will be able to find a 'way in' for this different child.

Flexischooling can redress this balance. Here the parent is giving dedicated time to the child with an ASD and, just as importantly, there is structure and support for what they do together. Perhaps they are working on formal learning tasks set by the school. Perhaps they are exploring a project of the child's own choice, be it visiting the recycling centre to see where the rubbish goes or spending many hours travelling the underground system. Whatever they are doing during this time together, there are opportunities for the relationship between parent and child to grow and mature.

Most psychologists will agree that the emotional link with the parents, perhaps particularly with the mother, is hugely important to the development and well-being of a child. Flexischooling gives more opportunity for this relationship to develop, and indeed gives it a context in which to develop.

The learning structure can be carried over into everyday life

It can be very difficult for the child with an ASD, used to the regulations of Monday to Friday at school (however unhappy this experience may be), to switch over to lack of structure at weekends and, worse, holidays. Holidays also bring their own problems. Many take place around festivals, when normal routines, mealtimes and family rules seem to change, visitors arrive, trips away are taken and, generally, most reassuring structure and predictability may be lost. For the child with an ASD, this can all be most unsettling and his behaviour may deteriorate worryingly at these times.

If the parent has already established a habit of structured learning through home-education time, it can be of huge benefit. Perhaps parent and child continue to have their quiet maths lesson each morning or to read their set book together in the afternoons. Perhaps they have some dedicated quiet time researching on the computer, or continue to work on their current project. Although this might sound as if the child with an ASD is missing out on the 'downtime' of holidays enjoyed by his neurotypical peers, in reality such 'downtime' may be the last thing he needs. Instead, the structure of having set, familiar and predictable routines may make the excitement and holiday visits, of Christmas, Thanksgiving, Eid or Hanukkah just that bit easier to take.

Lack of social exhaustion leads to greater opportunities to experience different social situations

The experience of the child coming home from school to slam up to his room for the evening highlights another problem with the strain that full-time classroom schooling puts on the child with an ASD. For this child, just getting through each school day is challenge enough. He has little energy left for trying any other experiences and apart from school (where he may well be totally isolated anyway) he may have very few opportunities for social interaction.

Flexischooling allows for less exhaustion. Perhaps he manages a morning in school, followed by a walk with his mother and the dog in the woods and a quiet afternoon of self-directed study. By the evening he is relaxed and ready to take on new challenges. Perhaps this is joining a Scout group, learning to trampoline, singing in a choir or taking part in a laser fighting challenge. There are tremendous opportunities for interest and social groups and these need not be age-orientated in quite the same way as school. Perhaps the child with an ASD feels happier working with adults at a local history group or as a volunteer with much younger children at a parent and toddler group. Many of these possibilities would just not be options if merely getting through the day is challenge enough (and there's still homework to get through!), so flexischooling can allow far greater social interaction possibilities simply by not making school the only option.

School-initiated interventions can be practised at home giving consistency across environments

Autism and Asperger syndrome are no longer new or unheard-of conditions and it is no longer necessary for the parent newly facing a diagnosis to do so alone. Most schools will have had any number of children with a similar diagnosis through their system before. Most individual teachers will have built up a wealth of expertise, and many teaching and learning support assistants will have attended numerous courses on offering support to these children. This is expertise the parents newly facing diagnosis need, and flexischooling can give them an opportunity to access it.

Perhaps the school has introduced a visual schedule to help a young child with an ASD to manage his day. This might involve a picture to indicate circle time at the top, followed by a book to indicate reading, some numbers to indicate number work time and then a beaker to indicate snack time. Staff might work very hard to support the child in learning how to use this schedule to make sense of his school day, taking each symbol off as the activity finishes and filing it in the 'done' box.

If the child is flexischooling, there is a great opportunity to continue the same schedule, with the same symbols and the same layout, at home. The child brings the schedule home when collected at lunchtime, the parent puts up similar symbols as appropriate (these might now include a visit to the park, the library, the swimming pool or Granny's house), and the child operates it in the same way. Consistency of approach in this way can be of tremendous benefit.

Of course, it works both ways and with the concept of 'shared responsibility' inherent in the flexischooling model, schools may be more willing to accept and adapt techniques introduced at home that can work in the school context too. Health and ASD experts can introduce suggestions in one setting and have every hope that they will be used consistently across both. Flexischooling really can allow for the best of both worlds to reach both worlds, and for these two worlds to be – as far as is possible – just the one.

Specific learning supports can be accepted and practised

School is a place of learning. A great deal of emphasis is placed on the social and behavioural learning of the child with an ASD, and this is understandable. Autism, as defined by Lorna Wing's triad of impairments (Wing and Gould, 1979) is a difficulty in social interaction, social communication and social imagination. These social impairments are manifested by behaviours that can be observed and which lead to the diagnosis of an ASD.

If a child with an ASD did not behave differently, it is unlikely he would have got a diagnosis in the first place.

However, it is not the behaviours that 'are' the ASD. Even if a child with an ASD managed to behave in an utterly unremarkable way throughout his time at school, he would still have an ASD. Too much emphasis on modifying the behaviour of a person with an ASD misses the point.

Even if flexischooling allows a situation where the child with an ASD manages to 'behave well' in school, his ASD still needs to be addressed. The way he perceives the world is fundamentally different. How he interprets the world through his five senses and through language is fundamentally different. His academic learning style, it follows, is likely to be different too.

This side of the development of the child with an ASD needs to be fully supported, and this may be extremely difficult to do within a busy classroom setting. Perhaps he needs specific interventions. Perhaps he cannot read, or (more commonly) cannot write. Does this mean he cannot understand? Academic support should look at finding ways around his specific difficulties as well as helping him with them. Specific interventions– with, for example, handwriting– are going to work best if there is considerable input. Flexischooling allows more hours to put in the necessary time, and this is one great advantage. However, it also allows considerable 1:1 observation by someone (the parent) uniquely motivated to get to the bottom of the child's needs.

He has a time to explore his own ASD
and manage, use and appreciate it

One of the most important aspects of education for the child with an ASD is that of learning who he is – ASD and all. School time gives him the opportunity to try out challenges and environments, without the fear that there is no alternative if he cannot cope. Home time gives him the opportunity and the privacy to explore what his ASD means for him. Although this is a somewhat controversial view, I believe there is much to celebrate in having an ASD. While much is made of the need to coax the individual into enjoying the social, external world around him, so equally I believe that he should be allowed to explore his own powerful inner world and interests. Flexischooling allows for both, and respects the need for both in the individual's life.

Winning all round

Perhaps the great thing about flexischooling is that it allows for success. So much of the life of the child with an ASD may seem focused around what he can't do, what he struggles with and failure. In order to get the diagnosis, he will have had to display deficits and difficulties, impairments and developmental delays. Similarly, unless he cries or screams, lashes out or runs away, his experience of school would probably have been deemed to be 'fine'. Unless he is actively unhappy, and finds a way to express this, it is unlikely that anyone will have been too concerned. It is as if the diagnosis presupposes low expectations: 'He has autism, what do you expect?'

Flexischooling allows him to step out of the system a little and for everyone to look harder at what he is doing. A shorter time at school can be an actively successful time, even an enjoyable one. If he is in school just for the parts he is happy with there is every chance he can do very well indeed. If he is only there for as long as he can concentrate on the real world around him and remain 'present', there need be no suggestion that there is anything 'wrong' with him. If he can maintain high self-esteem, who is to say that his rather unusual outlook can't be seen as positive?

Your experience of school days and of growing up in general can have a tremendously important impact on how you view yourself for the rest of your life. Flexischooling reduces the school experience to short but positive chunks. There is no need for failure.

Flexischooling allows the child with an ASD to practise being happy. It can give confidence as he builds on success and it can bring a great sense of achievement and of self-identity. Just as importantly, it can provide a prototype for the way forward into adulthood. Flexischooling allows for greater autonomy and less reliance on the 'system'. The pupil learns to study alone and to take greater responsibility for his learning. He learns to choose his own path, one that he can manage for himself and with good understanding of what that might be. This leads to a higher level of understanding of his own needs, which can be articulated at a higher level of study or in the workplace.

Nor are there any losers. Flexischooling empowers the child, but it can also empower the parents and the professionals at school. The child with an ASD is not the only winner. From the school's point of view, the staff benefit from having a relaxed, undisturbed, 'well-behaved' pupil who is not causing disruption to lessons or to other pupils. For the parents, flexischooling allows a structured, supported way of caring for the needs of the 'different' child while still being able to share that care with other professionals. The flexischooling approach, when it works best, empowers everyone. No one needs to feel the frustration of failing the child, and everyone—through shared responsibility and understanding – can 'get it right'.

Summary

- A happy child is a successful child. It is important to 'practise' being happy.

- Problems only overwhelm if they aren't dealt with. Flexischooling gives the opportunity to work issues out.

- School and family working together gives both support and a shared sense of care.

- Increased time for parents and child to spend together gives each a better chance to get to know (and really appreciate) the other.

- The child with an ASD, who will become an adult with an ASD, has a chance to be fully involved in his own development.

- School is (actually) just one small part of life. Flexischooling gives a more realistic perspective and means that the rest of life can be experienced and enjoyed.

Chapter 2

Setting it Up

Chapter 1 gave many examples of why flexischooling might work for the child with an ASD. So how can it be made to happen? What are the practicalities to setting it up and how, exactly, can it be made to work?

Persuade the school to consider it

As I said in the introduction, anyone – in theory – can set up flexischooling, if they have the time, energy and belief in themselves and their child, and if they can persuade the school to agree. Flexischooling is not a right, but is an arrangement made between parents and school for the agreed good of the pupil. In order to create a flexischooling situation you will need to persuade the school (usually the head teacher, principal or governing body) that what you are suggesting is going to be the best option, for your child and for the school. This may be no easy task.

For a start, the school will have its own approach to managing pupils with an ASD and other differing educational needs. Your first job is going to be to persuade the school that you are not rejecting these supports nor saying that they are inadequate or that they don't work. You are merely suggesting an alternative.

You may come up against some considerable resistance. It is not surprising if the school is defensive and views what you want with suspicion. The teachers and support staff may have spent considerable time setting up supports in school for all children and are probably very proud of the work they have done. It is essential that you do not get into conflict with the school about their way of doing things. For flexischooling to work it has to be a *shared responsibility* and you are going to have to find a way to work together.

Decide which school

Which school are you going to approach to work with you on flexischooling? If your child is already of school age then you may choose the school he is already attending, or you may decide to 'start afresh' at a new school. Much will depend on how things have gone before. If your reasons to consider flexischooling include the complete breakdown of relationship with your child's current school, this may not be the best place to start. Flexischooling demands a team effort, with home and school working together with trust and mutual respect.

Establish that you are not rejecting the work that the school is already offering

Whichever school you approach to suggest flexischooling, you are not, essentially, saying that anything they are offering already is wrong or unwelcome. Rather, you are saying that you fully appreciate everything that the professionals in that school are doing and, in fact, appreciate this work so much that you are prepared to dedicate large portions of your own time to supporting it and helping to make it work. All schools tend to stress that parental support is essential if the work they do is to be successful. They should, therefore, be pleased that you are offering to give dedicated time to this help and that you are taking the issue of your child's education with them so seriously. You are not removing your child to 'do it better', but instead are putting in the time to give additional support and to help to make what they are doing in school work as well as possible.

Establish that you are offering something extra

You will need to confirm how you will provide evidence that your child is learning (and what he is learning) during off-site time and to articulate clearly just what this 'extra' learning actually is. Whether this is appreciated will depend enormously on how far the person you are dealing with understands ASDs. If that person really does understand the needs, vulnerabilities, strengths, challenges and differences that come with having an ASD, it is probable that you won't need to explain very much. It is clear to most people who 'get' ASDs why flexischooling will work so well. On the other hand, if you are dealing with someone who does not have this understanding you may have an uphill struggle. You could start by explaining the situation, as outlined in Chapter 1 of this book. There are many reasons why flexischooling works, and if you are clear about them you are going to be in a stronger position. You may well still face reluctance and disbelief. See Chapter 4 for some further comments on this.

Reassure the school that its day-to-day work will not be disrupted

A school functions as a unit and if you are going to be doing something different to the norm you need to provide reassurance that this will not impact on this unit. Most staff in most schools are already stretched to the limit. What they will need is to be reassured that what you are suggesting will give them more support, not involve extra work. You need to be clear and to repeat often that what you are suggesting will *support* the work of the school, not be in opposition to it. You are not suggesting an alternative education; rather you are committing your time and resources towards making the education that the school already offers work better for your child.

Understand the school's concerns and be clear on the facts

You will need to understand how the school works and what the hidden priorities of the leadership team might be. Is it driven by results? Is it concerned about the place the school achieves in a league table? Is it worried about recorded absences, or by implications for funding? Clearly, these questions will have different answers depending on the country and/or county where you live, but it is advisable that you arm yourself with the facts before you start.

Reassure the school that you will work with them on everything that is important to them. You are choosing to send your child to this school, so you must believe in the school's ethos. If you were 'anti' the school, you would not entrust your child to it, even for part of the time. Reassure and repeat that you see your role as supporting your child to understand and succeed at the school. Explain how your child's time at the school will be improved, how he will be supported to be a 'good pupil'. Listen to the school's concerns about exams and disruption and take the time to take these concerns seriously. Successful flexischooling takes compromise and teamwork, negotiation and continued discussion and it is you, the parent who is requesting something different, who needs to lead that. Remember that in offering you a flexischooling arrangement the school is, in effect, extending you a courtesy. Be gracious!

Work out how to record the 'full-time education'

A full-time education is learning that goes on all the time. For the child with an ASD, this most certainly includes elements relevant to his ASD. It also, of course, includes academic learning. You and the school need to be very clear about who is responsible for what, and will need a flexible and easy-to-keep method to record what learning is taking place and when.

Decide on initial priorities

These may be fairly formal (to learn to read, to recognise number facts, to gain the understanding needed for an 'A' grade in physics) or may be far more informal. Perhaps your initial priority is simply that your child is happy and relaxed during his period of time in school, that he becomes more confident socially or that he learns to relax and use strategies to cope with stress. Particularly if he is returning to school on a part-time basis after a disastrous earlier experience, just building his confidence is a very valid initial target.

Agree on behaviour

One of the biggest challenges for the child with an ASD is to understand the various behaviours needed over different contexts. At home he just goes to get himself a drink of water; at school he has first to seek permission. At home he prefers lying on his stomach to read; at school he has to sit up in a chair at a table. Whatever issues are causing difficulty at school, try to be consistent and to use your additional time to practise them at home. Agree with the school on the naming of things. Is it called 'going to the bathroom', 'going to the toilet', 'being excused', 'taking a comfort break'? My grandmother used to call this 'spending a penny', which is a quaint (but deeply confusing) phrase. On the whole, the world for the child with an ASD is a great deal simpler if we all agree to call things what they are and do our best to be consistent – and that needs shared knowledge and agreed content.

Agree a format

The simplest way to record full learning across the two parts of a flexischooling day is a diary. This needn't be complicated. A notebook that goes into school and home again can be used to record what activities have been undertaken and what learning was targeted. This needn't be massively detailed, but should avoid 'gaps'. If the pupil comes home from school at lunchtime, his afternoon activity should appear in the diary. This may be completing the worksheets set in school, undertaking an online lesson or writing an essay. On the other hand, it may be going for a cycle with you in the park, having some quiet 'recharge' time by himself or, indeed, having a sleep. The idea is less to justify the activity and more just to record it. Only if the child's working week is recorded can his wider learning, and wider needs, be assessed.

Be flexible and review often

The last thing your child needs is for anything to be set in stone. Perhaps initially he was in school on Monday afternoons because the class did nature study; now they have switched to singing, which he finds distressing. If so, try to adapt and alter his hours. Equally, perhaps he used only to stay until break time on Tuesday mornings, but as he has become older and more confident you feel he could manage the whole morning. Try to keep the dialogue open with the school and with the teachers involved. If something is best for your child, it is always worth trying. It is also important to note that if it is better for you (do you need a full morning off?), or for the teacher in question, it is also worth considering. This is a team effort, and the more you can work together and help each other, the better for everyone.

Summary

- Keep it simple!
- Agree a short-term plan.
- Agree your contact person and work to establish a relationship.
- Get into school yourself if you can.

- Be courteous and gracious – flexischooling is not a 'right', and you need to work with the school to establish how it is in your child's best interests.

- Keep time in school short and successful...for everyone.

- Agree an easy-to-use and positive homeschool record and don't overdo it!

- Remember to thank and praise – teachers need reassurance and positive reinforcement too.

Chapter 3

Making it Work

Practicalities: keeping him safe

Your biggest priorities are the simplest. How will you, and the school, keep track of your child? Will it be absolutely clear at all times who has responsibility for him? If there is a fire alarm at school, will they be sure whether or not he should be accounted for? Other concerns need to be addressed too. What will you say when asked about his provision? If another student or parent feels that flexischooling is unfair, how will this be managed?

Establish a clear, 100 per cent reliable method for establishing where your child is and when

The easiest for this is a method of signing on- and off-site. Whenever he arrives at school, you sign him in. He never leaves school unless you sign him out (or, for the older child, unless he signs himself out). This needn't be time consuming or arduous, but it is absolutely essential you get this right. Any casualness or 'woolly' thinking in this area could lead to disaster and, at the very least, is going to undermine the validity of flexischooling from the start.

Agree what he/you/the school are going to say about your flexischooling arrangement

One of the objections often raised about flexischooling is a concern about what the other pupils will think and say. In reality, I have seldom known this to raise any major issues. Children accept that people do different things. Some children go out of school for medical or orthodontic appointments, for religious or cultural occasions, for family celebrations or because of family breakup. If your child is confident about his diagnosis (and why shouldn't he be? There is nothing wrong with having an ASD!), he will give this as his reason and it is likely to be accepted by his peers. Children are egocentric: if your child goes off-site because of his ASD that rules out the possibility of doing the same for most children, so they are unlikely to be too interested.

Other parents are more likely to cause an issue than the children. Most parents will never have considered the possibility of flexischooling and when they become aware of it some may try to instigate it for their child, for any number of reasons. Schools can be very concerned about this ('If we let you flexischool, they'll all want to do it'). In fact, this is a non-argument. Each application to flexischool has to be considered on its own merits. If other parents are merely 'jumping on the bandwagon' without proper reason or consideration, it is easy enough to turn them down. If they do have an equally valid argument and approach, of course, why not consider their request? Well-managed flexischooling will always help out a school, even if a number of families are offering it.

Given some schools' sensitivity on the subject, though, it may be best to discuss with the head teacher what your 'line' will be when other parents ask you. I have always favoured telling the truth, but not necessarily volunteering too much information. If it causes any interest at all, flexischooling is likely to be a bit of a 'nine-day wonder' and in a remarkably short time your child's slightly unusual school approach is likely to be fully accepted and forgotten.

Agree what constitutes 'success'

What do you want?

This is not as easy a question to answer as it may seem at first glance. When you have a child with an ASD you have to rethink many things. What is 'education' for a child with an ASD? Do you want him to succeed academically, to fit in socially, to learn more acceptable behaviour, to be independent, to accept and understand his own condition? How much of this is the responsibility of a mainstream school and how much is the responsibility of his home environment?

This needs to be agreed, quite specifically, with the school. Take, for example, his behaviour. If he lashes out at another child, is that the responsibility of home or school? Most schools would impose sanctions for this behaviour and expect those sanctions to be supported from home. But what if he lashes out because the school is failing to differentiate for his ASD? It is easy to see how home and school can come into conflict.

With flexischooling it is possible to set up a situation where responsibility for behaviour, as with so much else, is shared. Together, school and home can agree realistic targets, always building on success. As well as working on 'what not to do', you can get to the bottom of why the behaviour occurs, how to avoid it and what alternative behaviour would be preferred.

Equally, it may be the case that your academic expectations for your child and the school's expectations do not immediately tally. Children with an ASD often have a very uneven academic profile, being very good at some areas and very weak in others. Often this can be both frustrating and confusing. For example, a child with an ASD may have little ability to recall multiplication facts and struggle to add even single numbers in his head, yet be able to 'see' algebraic or geometric solutions to questions well beyond his years with apparent ease. Guiding such a child through a mainstream classroom is a teacher's nightmare, especially if the parents are in the background demanding to know why their high-IQ child is failing at the basics. Again, the answer is to work together, sharing the challenge, avoiding any suggestion of a blame culture and agreeing together on how to help his weaknesses while supporting his strengths.

The greatest strength of flexischooling when you get it right is this element of teamwork – where everyone is working together across the different environments of the child's life to give him the best possible education. As a parent, being part of a team that is working for the best for your child is a wonderful feeling.

Sometimes, parents of a child with any kind of special need feel very alone. Sometimes, indeed, the school's very 'expertise' can seem to exclude you. The school may decide what your child can and cannot do, how your child should be treated, whether your child is achieving his potential…even what your child's potential might be. Often, with an ASD, the school will introduce any number of initiatives around your child's behaviour. These might be very good and very successful, but it is hard as a parent not to feel 'out of the loop', and that your priorities for your child's development and welfare are not necessarily shared.

To give an example: Polly, who has an ASD and attends a mainstream primary school, runs away whenever it is time to wash her hands in the school bathroom and if she has to do so, she cries, screams and lashes out. The assistant working with her writes her a story explaining why it is important to wash her hands before eating and introduces a reward card where Polly receives a sticker each time she successfully washes her hands. The assistant works very hard, day after day, on a firm but consistent approach ensuring that Polly does indeed wash her hands with the other children. After many days of screaming and crying, the school report that Polly is 'making less fuss' about the handwashing. Everyone seems to be pleased but, as a parent, you are worried. Polly uses very little language, and your instinct would have been to use her crying as a communication opportunity. Why is Polly reluctant to wash her hands at school? Is she afraid? Is there some sensory issue in the bathroom? Polly has no issue with washing her hands at home, so it is a puzzle. Surely, her crying is an attempt to communicate and if someone could take the time to work out with her what she is trying to tell them, this would encourage her to communicate again. Polly is clearly communicating that she does not want to use the sinks in the bathroom, so would it be so dreadful to allow that communication to be successful, and allow her to use the ones in the classroom near the painting table instead?

Staff in schools are busy people, and their agenda will tend to be to find a way to get the child to 'fit in' and to behave in the same way as the other children. In this example, the assistant is working hard to get Polly to stop crying and objecting, but in doing so she may not be seeing the bigger picture. Indeed, in all probability she would say that it is not her business to do so. Her job may indeed be more about getting Polly to fit in with the class and to stop disrupting the handwashing routine established with the other children than about working on facilitating Polly's communication. Does facilitating communication for a child with an ASD come into the mainstream syllabus? Is the assistant trained to do it? Surely if she were, she would be being paid more than the rather paltry sum she is likely to be receiving. For the parents, though, Polly's communication is far more important than whether she uses one tap rather than another (they do not, after all, have a further 29 children waiting to wash their hands). Their instinct is to recognise the communication even if it means accepting alternative behaviour while the school is busy getting Polly to adapt her behaviour, even if that means ignoring her communication.

There is a genuine issue here about responsibility for the learning and development of a child with an ASD, about parental choice and parental responsibility. Parents sending a child into a school are generally expected to accept that school's ethos and to support staff efforts to teach their child. However, issues in mainstream schools about what that teaching may be concerning the 'autism' part of a child with an ASD may genuinely never have been considered.

Flexischooling gives a solution. If Polly goes home before the time when the problem incident is occurring, the immediate issue of 'but everyone has to wash their hands before dinner' is resolved. Meanwhile, her parents can work with her, supporting her to wash her hands in as many different contexts as possible and working with the communication opportunities these present. They can encourage her to wash her hands at home, in every available sink. They can go to relatives' houses and to visit friends, to public bathrooms and to restaurants. During flexischooling at-home hours they have the time and the motivation to do the detective work and to do everything they can to respond to Polly's communication. What causes her to baulk? Is it certain taps, certain smells, certain lights?

The answer to this real-life example was, in fact, that Polly was afraid of the hand driers, which seemed to come on like magic whenever anyone went near. When her parents realised this they were able to show Polly how they worked, introduce them to her gently and overcome her fear. She was then able to wash her hands at school without further problems.

Curriculum content and examinations

Many parents ask, 'Will my child still be able to take his exams if he flexischools?' The answer is yes, of course he will, if you want him to. Like most elements, this is one that you need to work out with your school. It will also, of course, depend a great deal on your child's personal abilities and preferences.

You may feel that the pressures and competitive element of many examinations are unhelpful to your child. If so, you are, of course, particularly well placed as someone who already flexischools, to withdraw your child on those days or for those sessions. On the other hand, many children with an ASD relish exam situations, with the quiet, the structure, the emphasis on facts and knowledge, and for these children exams can be taken as usual. Indeed, it is quite possible that your child may take *more* exams than his peers. As the child gets older he may find that he wishes to follow his interests independently, and you may find yourself entering him as an external candidate (one taking an exam not taught by the school) for any number of extra subjects. Again, flexischooling gives the time and the opportunity to do this.

It is worth mentioning, though, how important exam results are to many schools. This is understandable: the school may find itself judged by the outside world very much on these percentages, pass rates or grades. Sometimes the school may need your child to sit a certain exam in order to fulfil these kinds of pressures. Sensitivity to these issues will mean that your working relationship with the school is better if you listen to them, rather than if you blunder on with an attitude of 'I don't see why he needs to do this.' Talk to the school and try to come up with solutions together that are best for your child, both now and into the future.

It is also important to work with the school around examination and assessment support. The school may be able to apply to gain your child extra time in tests, or perhaps the right to take breaks or to use a scribe or a computer. Schools know a great deal about assessments – it is one of the things they do best. You will probably do well to work with them on what is best for your individual child.

Extra-curricular activities

In school/out of school

Of course, there are other elements to school than exam subjects and for many of us, looking back at our school days, these 'extra' elements stand out as the most important. Whether this was taking part in a school play, playing sport for the team, learning to make pottery mugs, playing the cello in the orchestra or nearly blowing up the lab in science club, these are the parts we all often remember.

For the child with an ASD, these 'extra' activities may be hugely important but they may also, for many, be missed. For the full-time student, the exhaustion of coping with the compulsory parts of school may mean that for the individual with an ASD, the idea of staying voluntarily to do yet more is inconceivable. He may be staggering home after an overwhelming day, with homework to do and work to finish, and all he may want is some quiet and peace to recharge. For such a child, all extra activities, both school based and in the community, may be simply beyond him.

Many people regard flexischooling as 'missing' various elements of school, but this need not be the case. It is quite possible that the child who has had the afternoon at home quietly recharging may in fact be prepared to return to school for an after-school club, or may be prepared to go out in the evening to a community activity. Reducing the intensity of the regular school experience may actually allow the child with an ASD who flexischools greater opportunity for social interaction and involvement.

For many pupils with an ASD, the most important element of extra-curricular activities in school lies in the fact that these clubs provide a safe haven during the unstructured periods of the day – usually break time and lunchtime. Having an activity to attend may make the dangerous wilderness of these times far more acceptable, to the point where these clubs may almost become unofficial 'social support' clubs for more vulnerable pupils. Where this is the case, the pupil who flexischools may still choose to attend during these times in order to access these groups. There is nothing about flexischooling that says he *cannot* attend any part of the day and his flexibility should mean the maximum chance that he does gain some social involvement from his school years. Remember to work with the school and, as always, to listen to concerns. It may be that it causes resentment with other pupils if your child appears to take up a valued place when they are not able to do so. Be diplomatic. For flexischooling to work, the elements of parents, child and school must be in harmony, and school is made up of many parts. The senior management team may be convinced it is working, but it helps if everyone – including the other pupils – see it as fair and positive.

What about school trips?

Flexischooling gives you that most useful of elements for the child with an ASD: flexibility. You will know best whether your child will enjoy a certain school trip, whether he will find it overwhelming and the prospect will cause him undue stress, whether he would enjoy part of it but will become exhausted by the whole...or any number of possible scenarios. The flexibility that is already written into his educational approach means that you can tailor these trips to suit him. He may not go at all (after all, staying at home to work is nothing new to him), he may go for the morning but be collected at lunchtime or he may enjoy the whole day if you are able to take the extra time beforehand to prepare him, perhaps visiting the site yourselves first. The same approach is true of residential trips. See Chapter 4 for further thoughts on these.

Summary

- Try to allow home time to support in-school time as much as possible.

- Be positive with your child: provide lots of praise and tangible rewards.

- Don't despair if it is running your life: it will probably settle down in time.

- Build gradually through the year but be aware of having to start again with each new academic year.

- Be alert and sensitive to issues such as exams, school presentations, school inspections, etc.

- Agree with the school the strategy for what to tell other parents...and generally keep your head down if this seems the best policy.

- Don't get into confrontation. The idea of flexischooling includes not needing to get stressed if the school don't always get it right. Be a diplomat!

- Keep your ears open for additional opportunities – after-school talks, clubs, etc. – and for ways you can help the school. Could you help run an after-school club?

- Keep reviews positive and build gradually for the future.

Chapter 4

Facing the Critics

Challenges you might come up against

You may need to be pretty thick skinned if flexischooling is the course you take. You may know that your child is happy, confident, achieving well and maintaining his self-esteem because of the support you are putting in, but unfortunately there will always be people who see how well he is doing and ask, 'So, what's the problem?' Worse, some of these people may attribute the remaining signs of an ASD, particularly lack of social interaction and under-developed communication skills, to what you are doing. To these people, you don't flexischool because your child is different, but your child is different, they believe, because you flexischool.

This can be very hurtful and frustrating, but you just have to hold on to the fact that your child is doing well. Over 70 per cent of children with an ASD suffer additional mental health problems (Madders, 2010), and anxiety and depression are so common as to be seen by some people as symptoms of an ASD so that their absence leads the person to question the diagnosis. If what you are doing means your child is doing well, be confident that it is good for your child and try to avoid discussions about whether other ways would be 'better'.

For example, another pupil with a diagnosis of Asperger syndrome who was flexischooled – we can call her Helen – was in a year group of 12- and 13-year-olds who were going on a week-long residential trip to an activity centre. Helen was initially very reluctant about this trip, but when she saw the range of activities on offer, including horse riding, high ropes and archery, she said that she would like to give them a go. After some discussion together, her mother and she agreed that her mother would take a room nearby and that Helen would attend the centre during the week as a day student. This she did, being signed in to join her peers for breakfast, taking part in all the organised activities without additional support and being collected and signed out after the evening meal. Each evening Helen's mother checked with her whether she would prefer to stay to take part in the free-time session before bedtime, but Helen consistently chose to return to their room instead.

The staff on the trip, who did not know Helen well, saw a child who was confident in activities, was friendly and relaxed if a little aloof and who seemed to show little anxiety or fearfulness, indeed no symptoms that they recognised of Asperger syndrome. They did identify, though, that although she had been at the school for nearly two years, she seemed to have made no close friends. They saw her mother collecting her and so 'denying' her the peer bonding of the evening activities and indeed the experience of sleeping in the dormitories, and they jumped to the conclusion that the mother's behaviour – over-protective and neurotic – was what prevented Helen from integrating fully. Was it surprising, they wondered, that Helen was socially clumsy when she had such a peculiar mother?

In fact, Helen and her mother interacted very little in their evenings together during the week. Instead Helen's mother gave Helen what she knew was most needed: time to herself. Helen read, listened to recordings of a particular radio show (one of her special interests) and mostly 'went into herself'. After a full day of intense social demands she needed time to recharge, to 'be autistic'.

Helen's mother had to provide this service for her daughter as there was no provision for it – nor understanding of it – at the activity centre. Here all children were assumed to want to be together in groups. Indeed, the children were specifically instructed that they were not to wander around the site alone, but to stay in parties of three or more and to join in one of the various voluntary activities provided by the centre staff. For a child needing solitude to recharge, this situation would have been very challenging. What is more, as Helen's need to recharge became greater, so was it likely that her behaviour would have become less acceptable. She was likely to have struggled to find a group willing to accept her since she would not have been able to join in with what they were talking about nor, even, with what they were doing. As she tried to shut down and go into her inner world, so her peers' rejection of her and frustration with her would have increased. At a practical level, who wants someone in your quiz team who isn't even listening to the question, and what use is a baseball fielder who doesn't even see the ball coming towards her, much less make any attempt to catch it? On a social level, what group of girls will welcome someone who doesn't understand the complex social rules of teen gossip?

Having had the evenings to recharge, however, Helen was able to join in each day with the structured activities and was an enthusiastic if quirky member of the group. Her peers' acceptance of her was not over tested and she was even seen as a valuable member of the teams. The other students accepted that she went off-site each evening because they knew she had an ASD and they knew how different this made life for her. Only the adults in the group failed to understand.

Comments and responses

Those who do not understand ASDs, and for the moment they remain the majority in society, may well be quick to criticise. Here are just some of the challenges you might come up against, together with some suggested angles of response.

- It will make him more different. (No – his ASD means that he is different, flexischooling just respects that difference.)

- He's doing fine anyway. (Define 'fine'. Just because he's not disruptive doesn't mean he's not unhappy; just because he's quiet doesn't mean he couldn't be achieving so much more.)

- You are being over-protective. (I know my child and realise his vulnerabilities. Is it likely I would be suggesting all this if I didn't believe it were necessary for his good?)

- He won't be able to make friends. (His social isolation is due to his ASD, not to being part time.

Indeed, being part time may actually help with social acceptance.)

- He'll miss out on all the fun stuff. (What is 'fun' to the neurotypical child may be torture to the child with an ASD. Equally, what is boring to the neurotypical child may be great fun for the child with an ASD. One size does not fit all.)

- He won't learn to be independent. (To move from dependence on adults most children move first to dependence on peers and only slowly to independence. The child with an ASD may be denied this transition step. I need to be there to provide the safety net in the meantime. All that I am doing works towards independence – but independence is only achieved through self-confidence and self-reliance. Failure, bullying, misery and repeatedly not being able to cope never made anyone independent.)

- You are living his life for him. (No one tries to flexischool against a child's wishes! Perhaps they are the ones who are not listening.)

- The school understands children better than you do. (However great their experience with neurotypical children, children with an ASD *are* different and *do* have different needs. Most ASD experts recommend flexischooling as an excellent option.)

- Other children with an ASD are managing fine here. (Define 'fine'.)

- He has to learn to cope. (Yes, for himself. He will learn through succeeding, which is what flexischooling is aiming to allow. Too much failure never taught anyone anything except how to fail.)

- If we allow it for him, everyone will want to do it. (Only other parents of children with specific needs who are equally in a position to give up all or most work to dedicate to teaching their child. I doubt the school will be overrun...)

- It will disrupt the school's work. (No – we won't let it.)

- There's no need. (I beg to differ...)

A note on 'part-time' schooling

One common question is: won't missing parts of school have a negative effect on the child's education?

The truth is that there is nothing new about part-time schooling for the child with an ASD. If you spend any time shadowing these pupils, it is alarming just how much of the curriculum they are missing.

THE PUPIL MAY BE MISSING WHOLE CHUNKS OF LESSONS BECAUSE HE IS STRUGGLING WITH MECHANICS

One boy being observed missed the first ten minutes of a lesson when instructed to get out his history book. He rummaged through his bag repeatedly, without his teacher realising and without having the communication skills to indicate that he couldn't find it. In fact, his teacher still had it from the previous lesson, but by the time she returned it to him she had settled the other children down to work and the pupil with an ASD had missed the instructions. Another child spent one complete lesson following the first instruction given ('Divide your page in half') with mathematical precision, but again missed the instructions. Of course his teacher didn't mean 'in half', she just meant 'into two roughly equal columns', but that wasn't much help to him.

THE CHILD WITH AN ASD MAY BE USING QUIET LESSON TIME TO WITHDRAW INTO HIMSELF AND 'RECOVER'

Very often the child with an ASD in the class who is most likely to be described as 'managing fine' is, in fact, no longer mentally present. The ability of so many people with an ASD to 'zone out', or to go into the world inside their head, is remarkable and, indeed, enviable, but it doesn't help much with accessing schoolwork. The pupil who is silent and apparently listening attentively to what the teacher is saying may well, in fact, be experiencing some much-needed 'down time'.

THE CHILD MAY BE MISSING LESSON CONTENT BECAUSE HE IS EXCLUDED BY HIS PEERS

For 'group work' to be effective for all students, all members of the group must be included. The pupil with an ASD may find his ideas or contributions rejected, or may lack the communication skills to express them effectively. He may find the social demands of the group confusing and conflicting and may allow himself to drift away and to miss most of what is going on during a session.

THE PUPIL WITH AN ASD MAY CHOOSE TO LEAVE LESSONS

Many schools have a policy that, should the student with an ASD be feeling overwhelmed, he can request to leave the lesson and go to a quiet area already agreed – perhaps the library or the pupil support unit – to calm down. This works well as an alternative to the student becoming overwhelmed, possibly lashing out or otherwise becoming disruptive, but it does further disrupt his lesson time. Because it is *ad hoc* it may mean missing whole lessons or parts of lessons in an unplanned and unmanaged manner. There is no guarantee that there will be anyone to provide specific or appropriate support when he arrives at the agreed place, and his ability to access this quiet time may be restricted by the limits of staffing or funding. This type of provision is dictated rather negatively by what the pupil cannot do, rather than being put in place positively to help him achieve more.

THE PUPIL (AND PERHAPS HIS PARENTS) MAY ARRANGE SOME TIME AWAY FROM SCHOOL IN AN INFORMAL WAY

Many is the time that the pupil who is struggling at school develops hard-to-pin-down ailments. Perhaps he reports a stomach ache or perhaps he claims that he has a pain in his ear or head. Indeed, for the pupil with an ASD who finds moderating his own internal condition difficult, it may well be that the pain is real. How can the neruotypical person really know what it feels like to be overwhelmed by your ASD? A parent may suspect that the symptoms are caused as much by stress and unhappiness as by a bug, but may also understand that the child's need to stay at home is very real and so write the necessary sick note.

THE PUPIL MAY BE EXCLUDED

The most effective way to get yourself out of an intolerable situation is to lash out. Usually in a school situation this will result in a reduction in social demands and a chance for some peace and quiet. Perhaps you will be made to stand on your own in the corridor (what a relief!) or sent to sit outside the head teacher's study (even better). At best, you will be sent home, which is what you most need.

This is not to suggest that behaviour of this kind is conscious or deliberate, but it is indicating that the child is overloaded and it does produce the desired effect. Yes, later there are unpleasant consequences, but at the time itself it may be the only way for the pupil with an ASD to get his needs heard.

According to the NAS, children with an ASD are 20 times more likely to be excluded from school than their classmates. In their 2006 survey (Batten *et al.*, 2006), they found that one in five pupils with an ASD are excluded at least once. Two-thirds of those children with an ASD who had been excluded had received more than one fixed-term exclusion, and 16 per cent had been excluded more than ten times, or so many times their parents had lost count. Of children in the survey who had been excluded, a third had missed a term or more of school and one in ten had missed more than a whole school year over the last two years alone.

These exclusions and this quantity of time out of school show how often schools are struggling to meet these children's needs. Flexischooling – the positive decision to share the responsibility of education with the school – is so much more positive an option. If parents are willing to make this huge commitment of time, energy and expertise, why would schools not embrace their help with open arms?

Looking to the future: employment

The flexischooling model can flow seamlessly into adulthood. Many adults with an ASD report that their school years were unhappy because of bullying, isolation and overload, but they may still frequently regret their passing. School gives strong structure, where, for example, every Monday from 8.45am to 9.30am means science in Lab 3 with Dr Smith. When the school years have passed, especially if the person is then not able to move on into full-time employment (as is the case with 85% of adults who have been diagnosed with an ASD; Rosenblatt, 2008), he may feel ill prepared to manage his own time and resources.

However, flexischooling can provide a solution.

- An increasing amount of employment can be accessed from home, especially by those who have strong computer skills. Success at this will require exactly the same skills as the flexischooled student will have developed over the past 15 years.

- There is a model of success (part time/flexible) already established that can be reproduced in the workplace by an employer encouraged to do so.

- This success itself – academic, social and mental – means that the adult with an ASD who has had a 'successful' school experience is far more likely to continue with it into employment.

What about me? Parents and flexischooling

No one can suggest that this is an easy option for parents. In order to take on sharing the education of your child with an ASD with a school, you will be taking on a tremendous challenge. You will be restricting your own employment possibilities during these (potentially) 15 or so years, since you will need to be available to take on this education of your child when other parents are 'freed up' by sending their child into school. Economically, therefore, you are likely to be affected and emotionally you may feel yourself to be rather stuck between worlds. You will be seen as 'different' by the majority of parents who send their children into the system full time and, at the same time, possibly viewed with some suspicion by the full-time home educators who have rejected schools completely. While flexischooling remains a minority option you may find yourself having to explain yourself, although, as more parents choose to take up the option and flexischooling becomes more widespread, this should become less of an issue.

It is also, of course, well worth remembering that, although in some ways it may be tough, flexischooling can be a real joy. Your strengthened relationship with your child is likely to be reward enough and when flexischooling works and you can feel part of a team working together to help guide your child through a childhood with an ASD to successful maturity, then it really can be tremendous.

Part 2

FLEXISCHOOLING IN ACTION

Sam's Story

A Mother's Perspective on Flexischooling

What is flexischooling like in practice?

The best way to give an idea of this seems to me to give a real-life example. This is Sam's story of flexischooling and should give you a clearer idea of how this approach can work.

Each child with an ASD is different and each family situation is different. What is described in this account is by no means the only way of approaching flexischooling, but it should give some idea of ways it can be experienced and of how it can work.

And it is all true. Although some of the details have been changed, the positives and the successes are real. Most of all, the joyous and confident boy is real. 'Sam' really has been this happy and flexischooling really has worked this well for him.

Before school

At age four Sam had language, but little ability to communicate. He mostly quoted chunks of Thomas the Tank Engine stories and seldom asked for anything. Requests and direct communication were always very slow, and you could almost see the cogs whirring. Getting him to answer even the simplest direct question took immense patience and showed how fragile his communication skills were.

More immediately worrying, his attachment to us was fragile. He didn't stay by my side and would wander off, if allowed, showing no anxiety if he lost sight of me and no fear of getting lost. He wouldn't respond to his name being called and wouldn't look up to check if I were following him. He showed no joy at being reunited with his father or me after an absence, nor any distress at being left. After a while we came to the conclusion that he didn't see us as any different to anyone else. When being picked up from nursery, he had to be told which adult was 'his' and therefore whom to go home with.

Already at nursery his lack of cohesion to the group was obvious. The others would sit in a group; he would continue to play by himself unless physically positioned with them (he showed little understanding or response to verbal instructions). He spilt his milk, had no pencil control, couldn't thread the beads, failed to take any pleasure in putting paint on paper (he only ever put it at the bottom of one side anyway), and would then wander off. He could entertain himself with minutiae to an almost infinite degree -- pushing a train around a track, running a car over a wall, lying to watch a block topple, looking at a book. He would tolerate other children around him, and only became distressed if they invaded his space or if they picked up one of the pieces he was playing with. If this happened, he would not interact with them, but would swiftly and physically remove the object from the child (or the child from the object with a quick shove!). If this made the other child cry, he didn't seem to notice.

So – given this profile – why on earth did we ever think that sending him to school was a good idea?

There are many reasons, and some are quite complex. The most obvious is convention. I come from a world where children start school at the age of four years, so I didn't question that my child would do the same. His big sister was already passing through the system and this was familiar ground to me. Many of my friends were the parents of children of the same age. School rolled on, and it didn't seem an option to challenge it…

More than that, though, was my belief in that system. Before stopping work to have children I had been a teacher. I believed in school. I had never questioned that it was 'where children go'. Like the health service that had taken my blood pressure, offered me scans and told me my children were healthy, I didn't expect to question it. The health system passes the care of the young to the education system at the age of four. It was as simple as that.

There was also the secret belief that school would provide a solution – that within a few weeks of entering the production line of school, Sam, like his sister, would have magically absorbed the rules of society. I had seen it with her, and with other children. They enter the door on the first day as a bunch of individuals, milling around in an uncoordinated fashion with various quirks – from favourite toys to the need for a banana at 10am – and within a few weeks they have 'got it'. They line up, they face the same way, they dress themselves, they manage without a dummy or a huggy or a bottle or an afternoon nap. They get cleaned up and regularised and though it is a wrench to see it, as a parent, it is also a relief. There is a feeling of 'job done', of having delivered your baby into a system from which they will emerge in 15 years or so as a functioning, qualified, fully formed and successful adult.

As things were I was feeling increasingly isolated. I had dared, on occasion, to say that I felt my child was 'different'. This was hugely unpopular with the other mothers. All mothers, of course, believe that their child is different – special and unique – while holding on firmly to the equally held belief that he is 'normal'. There is a wealth of insecurity in parents, and none likes you to rock the boat by daring to voice concerns. If you do ('No, my child really *is* different'), it really isn't popular.

Faced with all of these elements, school seemed a good idea. I suppose that I knew, deep down, that Sam wouldn't magically fall into line when he walked through that door. Perhaps I felt that, as soon as they spent any time with him, the teachers at school would become aware of just how different he really was and I would have someone to help me to understand my child.

Sam starts school

I sent Sam into school…and watched him go under. I wasn't, of course, actually there, but the stories soon reached me. The children of my friends came home to their parents with tales of how Sam had had to go and stand by the 'thinking' wall, sit by himself, be sent back into the classroom, and be kept in at playtime. They told of how he had become lost when he failed to follow the rest of the class to the hall, shouted out in assembly, ran out of singing time, didn't come in from playtime when the bell went and had to be collected, 20 minutes later, when spotted by the school secretary still wandering around, alone, outside.

I went into school, of course, and tried to find out what was happening. What I saw was terrifying. This was a good school, with kind and dedicated staff, but when faced with behaviour they didn't understand they sought to eliminate it. What they did, in fact, was turn a happy, secure, 'different' child into an anxious, sensory-seeking and distressed one.

In that first term I watched Sam's problems – his 'differentness' – escalate. He started to spin – endlessly spinning round and round as fast and for as long as he could – every playtime, every lunch, in the hall, whenever he had the space. He also started to suck and bite. He would suck clothing, toys and his own hand, biting down on it with his whole hand sometimes in his mouth. He started to spit – spitting at other children, spitting streams of dribble onto the floor and playing with his own saliva. When made to sit in the prescribed 'cross legged' position he would fold forward and bang his head again and again on the floor. In assembly he would cover his ears and rock. His language use dropped away, becoming seldom other than repeated set phrases. He soiled himself repeatedly; he wet himself. He came home each day uncomplaining and quiet, and went into school each day, uncomplaining and quiet, but he began to develop routines. He had to touch certain objects before he left the house, and on the way to school he had to follow a certain path. When he arrived at school he would follow the same unchanging routine, going first to the sink and removing and replacing all the paintbrushes, then running his hands along the draining board, then picking up book after book from the book corner. From there he would be collected by the teacher and taken to sit down with the other children. Once there, his hand would go into his mouth and his eyes would glaze. I would leave him, according to his teacher, 'fine' and I felt frankly terrified.

After a term the school agreed that Sam was a little different in his behaviour. They would put a stop to most of this, they assured me, but they did concede that there may be a 'slight' issue. Perhaps he had glue ear and was having trouble hearing? They suggested I take him to the doctor.

I did.

After nearly two years of delays, cancellations and mistakes, our appointment finally came through with the specialist paediatrician. Sam's conditions had a name: he had autism.

Strangely, given the enormity of that diagnosis, I remember it with joy. It was like a whole load of white noise which had been going on and on in the background suddenly clearing. Autism. Yes, that made sense.

We took Sam out of school immediately.

Homeschooling

The move, apparently so momentous, was incredibly quick and easy. I had no doubts. Sam had autism. Our future had changed from that moment, and we needed to rethink so much. In the meantime, Sam was clearly in the wrong place. Having said that, it did take courage. I expected the sky to fall in. Take my child out of school? What would people say?

In fact, no one really cared. The school (although to be fair they didn't say so) were probably pleased to be rid of a potentially difficult child and an actually difficult parent! Other parents, whatever they may say, are not keen to have a pupil in their son or daughter's class who may take teacher attention away from their own child. Already their little ones were coming home with tales of 'What Sam did' and how the lesson was stopped to deal with it. I'm perfectly sure most of them were delighted to see the back of him.

And we were delighted to have him back. I will always feel I owe him an apology for that awful first experience of school. Now we made up for it. We were no longer fighting the health system to try to get to see an 'expert' for a diagnosis. We weren't fighting the education system and being racked with fear and remorse and anger. Instead, we stayed at home and played. We had long, long days where Sam and I just spent time together. We didn't go far; he played with his wooden trains and I watched him and learned about him. Gradually, I felt that I got to know this little boy who had been so perplexing to me. I realised that there was a reason, of sorts, for everything he did and that he wasn't acting randomly or disruptively, but with a different brand of good sense that he had found for himself.

We home educated Sam for the remainder of that year and well into the next. It was a time of great learning for us as a family. I attended many courses and gained various certificates and qualifications, and I started to put a variety of different recommended techniques into place to help support Sam. Some of these worked and some didn't. What they did do was to help me form the question: 'What does Sam need?'

This meant looking at what we wanted from his education. We came to realise that there was a lack of specialist support available for children with autism in mainstream schools. We were hoping for someone qualified, experienced, expert and professional who would be able to suggest and implement a whole host of supports suitable for Sam. We realised that such a person (and such a place) doesn't exist. What we were more likely to get would be some hours of support in a mainstream school from someone who might or might not have any autism qualifications or knowledge at all, indeed who might have very few professional or educational qualifications. We realised that it is a lottery. We would be fighting for some hours of adult support from a 'teaching assistant', but would have no say as to what that support would be or who would deliver it. We would have no say in ensuring that that support was for Sam and not, in reality, for the teacher.

Sam's needs

This seemed to us to be a huge difference. We wanted Sam's needs and difficulties addressed and remedied. We wanted someone who understood what these were, who would help put into place programmes to help him deal with them and help him move forward, and who would act as an interface between Sam and all of the parts of school life that would be confusing or unsuitable for him. What we didn't want was someone to 'manage' Sam so that he did not disrupt the other children's leaning. This would place far too great an emphasis on Sam's behaviour, yet so much of what we heard previously at school was couched in terms of behaviour. If Sam couldn't work quietly, he was taken out. Well, yes – we understood that. What we wanted was for the issue of *why* Sam couldn't work quietly to be addressed. Was it because the work itself was unsuitable, or unsuitably presented? Was it because he couldn't cope with the 'working together' aspect of the task but could quite easily finish the worksheet if allowed to do it alone? Was it because the fluorescent light in that classroom was flickering and making it impossible for him to concentrate, or because the instructions for the task were ambiguous, or because the sound of the radiator was grating on his teeth, or because he was terrified that at any moment the change-of-lesson bell would go off? Was it that his 'not working quietly' was his attempt to draw the teacher's attention to the fact that he needed to go to the bathroom, or was it because he lacked the necessary social skills to join in the group discussion? In only a handful of these cases would the presence of a second adult actually help Sam's situation. It was far more likely that that adult would be used to remove Sam to prevent disruption to the rest of the class.

What we didn't want was for Sam to go back into a school, only for the school once again to try to 'knock him into shape'. We didn't, we realised, want school to try to stop his autism, but instead to understand it. This was a much bigger challenge.

We were also worried because the remedies that Sam had come up with in his four-year-old way last time hadn't been listened to, but had been, to all intents and purposes, crushed. Spinning, sucking his hand, becoming absorbed in books had all helped him, but all were behaviours the school sought to stop. We wanted to take things that step further and ask *why* they helped and what were they trying to block out? In what way was the spinning helpful to Sam and what could we work with Sam to do that was as effective but more socially acceptable?

Most of all, we felt that Sam needed to spend his childhood years learning how to be a successful and happy adult with autism. The autism, if you like, was the constant; the childhood was not. So much in our society is geared towards meeting the needs and development of our children as they journey towards adulthood. Sam's journey from child to adult was going to be only part of the picture. He had to manage the autism for himself if the journey was to be successful.

We had started from a point where we had removed him from school to prevent the damage that school could do. Now we had moved on. Now we wanted more than to prevent damage – we wanted school to deliver something positive!

Starting to flexischool

With this in mind, we returned, very cautiously, to the school environment. The school he had originally attended, where his sister was still a pupil, was some distance away. There was another, much closer school, which we had initially rejected because the school buildings were old and shabby and its resources seemed scarce. Never judge a book by its cover! This turned out to be the most wonderful school for Sam.

Our first approach was when Sam was six. We made an appointment with the head teacher and discussed what we felt Sam needed out of school. Together we agreed that a flexischool approach was well worth a try. What we liked most about this arrangement was that we would be working together as a team, with Sam firmly at the centre and with the school and us as parents sharing the responsibility, the challenges and the joys that were his education.

We agreed that we would begin slowly. His period of home education had calmed him considerably and above all we wanted to keep Sam happy and relaxed. This wonderful head teacher (who became a close friend over the next four years) was completely open and flexible. She suggested that we follow Sam's lead, being patient and gentle and making sure that we never pushed him further than he was happy to go.

Initially, Sam was encouraged to explore the empty playground at the end of a school day after the other children had gone home. He was able to make a preliminary visit to get to see the basic geography of the school. He got to meet his teacher, look round and explore, have a go on the interactive whiteboard, check out the books in the book corner and visit the loos. That was it for that first day. The second visit, later in the week, was the same. His teacher again met him and let him set his own pace.

On the third visit we arrived earlier, during the school day and while the children in the class were out at afternoon playtime. This time, while Sam had looked around, the children started to come back in. His teacher asked him if he would like to stay sitting in the book corner for the story time and Sam agreed. On each of these visits I had stayed with him, and on this occasion I took him back out as soon as the story finished. We watched the other children being brought out by the teacher some few minutes later as the school day ended to find their parents. Would Sam like to try that next time?

So, in the second week of his new school journey, I took Sam into the classroom and left him with his teacher during afternoon playtime. He stayed without me for story time when the class came in, waited with them through the scrummage of collecting books, bags and coats (still in the book corner) and came out with them for home time. I collected him like any other 'regular' parent, and was able to ask him how his day went! I think we were both delighted with ourselves. Sam thought it was great and was keen to do it again. We agreed that this would be his routine twice a week, and we got ourselves settled into this pattern. Soon we took it as the norm – on Mondays and Thursdays Sam 'went to school'. This might only be for 15 minutes each day, but for that time he was happy and confident. This felt like a good start.

The next trick was to ease him back through the day, and to integrate him socially. The latter happened fairly naturally. Children accept that adults do odd things, and none of the children seemed to question their teacher's assertion that they had a new boy who only attended for a short time in the afternoons twice a week. Right from the start, his teacher told them – and Sam told them – that he had a 'special brain'. The issue of disclosure can be a difficult one, but we had been open with Sam that he was different from the start. He knows that his brain worked differently from most other people's and, indeed, is secure that it is better! By this stage, after diagnosis, he had undergone a whole battery of tests including a range of intelligence tests, all of which put him at considerably above average (in the 'superior' or 'very superior' range). We were lucky here, as knowledge of his intelligence has always been one of Sam's best defences against feeling that there is anything 'wrong' with him. He is proud to have autism, which he sees as an evolved brain and the way forward for the future of humanity. He sees himself as a trailblazer, and was quick to convince the other children

behind whichever child was at the front, and not to push in. That may not seem much, but for a child with autism it is a tremendous achievement.

Sam only managed playtime, the return to the classroom, story time and coming out for the remainder of that year. What he did do was improve the content of that time in school. He moved from staying in the book corner to sitting with the other children, from reading his own book to listening to the class book. He learned to respond to the playtime whistle, to line up, to go to fetch his coat and to change his shoes when asked. He learnt the name of his teacher and to identify her and was able to pick out me or his father in the playground at the end of the day. He learnt to remember to bring letters out from school and to hand them to us and to pass on simple verbal messages between his teacher and us ('Mrs X wants to talk to you'). To some people these might seem rather small achievements, but we knew they were huge. During this school year, for about half an hour twice a week, Sam enjoyed school, behaved appropriately, was polite and friendly and happy and needed no additional support. We were onto something!

Age 7–11

The start of the following year meant big changes. He was now in what is known in England as 'Key Stage Two' (KS2), which meant not just a change of classroom but that he occupied a different part of the school. This meant new routes, new cloakrooms and new loos. He had a new teacher and new classmates. How would he cope?

Initially, we went right back to basics. KS2 had no afternoon playtime, so Sam merely started at the end of the day and worked backwards. At first he arrived at school, went straight to the book corner and stayed there until it was time to come home half an hour later. This seemed like a step backwards but we decided to be patient. There was a lot of new stuff for him to learn.

He was blessed, once again, by having a wonderful teacher. Sam's positive experience of flexischooling is, in no small part, down to the excellent support that he has had from all of his teachers. It takes courage for a school to take on something as different and as untried as what we have been doing with Sam. I will never be able to express my gratitude to all the professionals we have been lucky enough to meet at Sam's schools who have had the faith to take it on, and who have made it work through their dedication, hard work, enthusiasm and initiative.

Once Sam was happy and relaxed in his new class (and his happiness in school, coupled with an expectation that he would always show the highest standards of politeness and good behaviour, were all we were demanding in his education plan), we were ready to challenge him a little more. After discussing it, we decided we needed to challenge him *more*, not just *longer*. His teacher came up with the plan of putting on a whole-class activity, which would happen for 20 minutes during the last half hour of the school day on the days when Sam attended. The activity was varied – sometimes it was a 'show and tell', sometimes it was learning a song, sometimes it was a discussion – but it was always something that did not rely on anything covered at any other time in the week. Sam, therefore, could join in on an equal footing, and gradually we expected him to do so. At first he was expected to join in as audience, but with attention. Then he was asked to join in as the main participant, bringing in something to present to the class. Gradually this developed to joining in with a class discussion, working in pairs and working in a small group. Sam found much of this very difficult, so his short school time did become a real challenge for him. During the 20-minute activity he was not permitted to 'opt out' or read, although he still started each session in the book corner and was allowed to return to it while the other children collected books, bags and coats at the end of the day. In this way, while respecting that he used books as his filter to block out what he couldn't cope with, the school also challenged him to push himself to try to cope.

One of the strengths of our scheme was that the school never tried to go too fast, too soon. What we had was a very small proportion of the school week when Sam was in school, but for that time he was receiving an education entirely tailor-made to his needs – something that would simply not have been possible were he there full time. During these sessions, his needs were never over-stretched but, because he was always challenged that little bit more to join in, to listen, to take in instructions and to interact, he learned a huge amount in these very small 'chunks'. Perhaps most important of all, his success rate was extremely high. Sam prospered. For a long time his hours at school remained constant, but Sam came on in leaps and bounds.

By the following year his teacher and I, hugely encouraged and excited by what we had come up with, started to work together to get even more out of his sessions. We realised that Sam did not know the names of his classmates – and then we realised that he did not seem to recognise any of them! He was unable to point out his teacher from his first year. When faced with a visiting priest to the school, he caused minor scandal (and some amusement!) by saying: 'I think that man is my Dad.' We realised that his ability to decode faces was very poor. Everyone had two eyes, a nose and a mouth, but he didn't seem to be able to tell one from another. It was hardly surprising if he failed to register subtle changes in facial expression and emotion!

With permission, we gathered together photographs of members of his class. I played games with him at home, games such as 'Snap' and 'Pelmanism', which required him to match and remember. In school, his teacher followed this up with name games, games where the children got into groups and activities around finding a partner and sorting into type by hair colour, eye colour, etc. Gradually Sam came to recognise some members of the class, and even to begin to express preferences. Although it was a long way off, he was making the first steps towards making active friendships.

Sam was thriving and his involvement in school was growing organically. He was beginning to see himself as a member of the class. When his class had trips out, he was able to go along (with me in attendance as a parent-helper, just to make sure). When his class were doing assembly, he was given a part, which meant that he was needed in school for practice time. When it was time for his class Christmas party, Sam chose to be part of it. He took a book and, indeed, chose to read it rather than join in some of the games, but that wasn't seen as a problem by anyone.

We had a meeting in school to discuss how to challenge him next and together we came up with two suggestions, both common 'stumbling points' for the child with autism. The first was to join in for sports lessons, and the second was to stay for lunch.

Sports require many skills that may challenge the child with autism. First, there is the business of getting changed, which requires a level of self-help, independence and the ability not to mind being jostled in an often rather small space as knees and elbows are shoehorned into shorts and t-shirts. Then it requires managing a large space, either a hall or gymnasium or the outdoors. Halls and gymnasia tend to be echoing and noisy places, and there may be little natural light. Instructions are almost always given verbally and shouted, and much may rely on the child's ability to mimic or copy either the teacher or fellow pupils. Most games require an element of teamwork. They may also require developed coordination skills and elements of physical contact. The rules may be confusing, just as the lines of many different types of court laid out on the floor may overlap and run together. Children may be encouraged to call out or yell instructions, and generally the atmosphere may be more 'robust' than in normal, academic lessons.

As before, heightened awareness of Sam's needs meant that solutions to problems were found before serious issues developed. After the first session when Sam stripped all of his clothes off, his teacher went for a very clear approach. Rather than the rather vague instruction to 'get changed', she instructed her class very clearly to remove specific outerwear (shirts, jumpers, skirts or trousers), to leave it on the chair, and to put on sportswear (t-shirts and shorts). She put pictures of the stages for this up at the front and indicated that she wanted them to have reached stage three by the time she had counted to 20...making it into a game. She was able to report that, not only did it work for Sam, but also it worked like magic at speeding up her whole class! Very often, solutions put in place to support Sam were found to be helpful to other pupils, and Sam's legacy has been a whole host of strategies in place that make school life simpler and easier for all.

This clarity of instruction giving, coupled with an acceptance that Sam does struggle to function in a large group like this, meant that sport could be termed a success. Sam may never have excelled in sporting terms, and may have only the haziest concepts of the rules of team sports, but he enjoyed it! That in itself was the huge achievement. A subject that has had children with autism turning into school refusers was, Sam opined, 'quite fun'. A year later he was even able, and happy, to join in for part of school sports day. The situation had been handled with great sensitivity and autism awareness, and Sam was never made to feel that this was something he 'couldn't do'.

Lunchtime threatened to be an even bigger challenge. The lunch hall is large, noisy and smelly. It provides a huge assault to the senses. For a child easily 'disgusted' by textures and tastes, it was a potential minefield.

The way round one set of problems was easy. Children could, if they wished, bring a packed lunch so it was decided that Sam would do so. This packed lunch was, every day, precisely identical. For the fortnight or so before he started eating in school, Sam had this same packed lunch, presented in a packed lunchbox. Initially he ate this at home. He became familiar with what was required to open the packets, manage the drink and so on, and was reassured that the lunch was always, as he said, 'delicious'.

Next, we started taking his packed lunch with us and eating it in a variety of different places. We ate in libraries and church halls, on park benches and in friends' living rooms. We ate where it was quiet and where it was noisy. We even managed to eat where it was 'smelly' by persuading his grandmother to cook a fish pie just before we went round to her house!

Separately, we tackled the issue of the hall. Sam was, understandably, reluctant. Looking at it from his point of view, it was noisy and apparently chaotic. There were queues of people moving in different directions; there was a completely different set of adults in charge, none of whom he knew. There were, inevitably, crumbs and spillages on the tables – gravy, custard and stray peas on the tables where the hot dinners were taken, smears from yoghurt lids and fragments of crisps on the packed-lunch tables. The level of chatter was exuberant and, what with chairs scraping on the floor, knives and forks clattering and plates being stacked, it certainly did assault the eardrums.

We reassured Sam that he wouldn't be expected to eat in there just yet, but in order to get him familiar with the environment his class teacher appointed him 'Water Monitor'. It was Sam's job to collect the water jugs from the tables, take them to the kitchen to be refilled and return them. This was a clean job, and one that appealed to Sam's sense of 'being helpful'. He didn't object, and for the last ten minutes of each lunchtime seemed happy with this task.

The problem of the tables being messy was easy to fix. Lunch was in two sittings. Sam was permitted to always attend the first sitting, when all was pristine and unsoiled. He ate his predictable, ultra-familiar packed lunch without a murmur, and at great speed. He then filled the remainder of the time (which his peers spent chatting) refilling and replacing the water jugs. This took him to the end of the 'sitting' and he was able to go out. All seemed well.

There were problems of course. Sometimes the lunchtime staff didn't put the tables out in quite the same place; once one of the staff reprimanded Sam for leaving his seat to do the water jugs; on a couple of occasions the smell in the hall was overwhelmingly strong so that he couldn't eat anything. Sam was never keen on the lunchtime experience, but was able, usually, to tolerate it and get some food eaten.

Sam seldom any longer displayed overt behaviours of autism – but he still had autism. This is an important point to note. Sam's autism means that his brain is different to that of a neurotypical person. He perceives the world differently: his sensory responses are different – he hears things I cannot hear and doesn't hear things I do, he sees patterns where I see none, and struggles to decode what I can recognise instantly (for example, a familiar face). He also understands differently, which gives him a strange, strange world. Watching drama on television with Sam is an eye opener. He believes what the characters say, and will believe that the villain is the 'good guy' long after it is reasonable to do so. He is also appalled by lying and will condemn a character who does so, however 'good' their motive. Given how he understands, it is not surprising that he prefers to watch factual programmes. He also reads mostly fact-based books, although he also hugely enjoys fantasy tales of dragons and knights, which have a clear-cut moral world of Good and Evil. It is only through spending time with Sam and listening in to his rather idiosyncratic reporting that the huge differences of his world become apparent. Sam is bright, articulate, intelligent and friendly, but he has autism. The school's acceptance of that was what made his flexischooling experience so successful.

Personally, I love the way Sam's brain works. I find it endlessly interesting to try to track back over confusions and anomalies and try to work out where the misunderstanding occurred. I even love it when, on visits to professionals such as opticians, he responds to questions like 'Can you read the top line?' with the simple (and truthful) response: 'Yes'. At such times, I am not laughing at him, but with him. He is as he is and is never going to change. What was a joy as he settled into his flexischooling experience was the feeling that I didn't have to guard against all these times, to protect him from the huge vulnerability his unusual processing could bring. His teachers had grasped completely what was going on. Here, at last, were other people who fully accepted Sam's difference, in no way sought to undermine it or 'treat' him for it, but were as interested as I was in finding ways of making it work for Sam. These teachers, because they were not overwhelmed by Sam since he was in school for only a short time, were ready to make adjustments, to accommodate Sam's autism and, above all, they weren't frightened of it. The joy for me of finding someone else who was as entranced as I was by the challenges we faced together was wonderful. His teachers and I became almost daily swappers of new pieces that made up the picture. 'Sam didn't write his diary today,' one teacher said. 'My fault! I saw he was reading and I said, "We're doing our diaries now, Sam." When, ten minutes later, I realised he hadn't moved, I thought back over it. Silly me! I can almost hear him thinking it: "You may be doing diaries; I'm reading!" I'll catch him next time!'

What I love about that exchange is the single phrase: 'My fault'. In it is the acceptance that Sam, the child, has a neurological difference, and it is for the teacher, the neurotypical adult, to make adjustment to accommodate it. That attitude, which gradually pervaded the whole school as more and more people – adults and children – 'got' what it was to be Sam, was, more than anything else, what made Sam's experience of school so successful. After all, it was not as though he were not adapting all the time. His sessions at school were kept short because it was exhausting for him to function in what was, basically, an alien environment. Of what went on around him in school, 99 per cent remained tailored for the neurotypical person. The environment itself, most of the communication that went on, the examples, the people (most of whom were still unrecognisable), were all things that Sam had to adapt to. That's life. Sam, as a person with autism, is in a minority and we live in a culture of majority rule. However, at last we had found somewhere that was willing, genuinely, to make what changes it could to make that environment more Sam-friendly. They accepted him, and accepted that he was worth adapting to. They liked him.

I think one of the reasons people were so ready to adapt to Sam was because of his engagingly open and friendly personality. He is a friendly boy – but why not? With our flexischool arrangement he was not frightened or feeling threatened, and was confident that he was in a situation with which he could cope. He was able to trust that adults would listen to him, and would be willing and able to help him.

As regards his peers, he maintained remarkably high status with them. Children can be very cruel. There is a pack instinct in all of us, but more obviously to the fore in the young, which seeks out and rejects what it sees as 'different'. Many people with autism have experienced rejection and indeed bullying because they are 'weird'. Their crime seems to be that they are pretending to be 'normal' (or, even worse, pretending to be trendy or 'cool'). Sam never disputed his 'weirdness'. Indeed, he championed the fact that he was different right from the start. Society doesn't seem to mind this. Indeed, many older teenagers and adults spend a great deal of time trying to cultivate their 'weirdness' and their ability to be different. Apparently the weird, the mad and the different are fine as long as they accept that they are. It's okay to say: 'Don't ask me; I'm a total nutcase!' Indeed, the people with the highest status in a society such as a school will almost universally be slightly unconventional. Sam's high status meant that he was never in any danger of being a victim. The girls tended to mother him and look after him. The boys accepted him and even deferred to him. In his final year at the school his classmates elected him to represent them on the school council. Clearly, they did not see his being part time as a disadvantage, nor, indeed, his autism. They saw a child who was unswervingly honest, who had an unnerving adherence to fairness and justice and who was never afraid to speak up for what is right. He made an excellent school council member.

Meanwhile, what did we spend our time doing for all those other hours and hours of the 'school' week?

Flexischooling at home

Flexischooling involves part-time attendance at school, not part-time education. This is an absolutely essential concept to grasp: when Sam wasn't in school, he was still required to be learning.

A great deal of Sam's learning during his 'at-home' time related back to school. We would unpick the various issues raised by his time in school and work on improving them. Perhaps the school had indicated that he had trouble queuing. Sometimes issues were quite specific (like having trouble recognising members of his class) and sometimes more general (having trouble waiting his turn). Whatever these social issues raised, Sam and I would then work on them in our at-home time. I used a great many autism-specific resources, and also a great deal of individual inventiveness! We might use a Social Story™ (see www.thegraycenter.org/social-stories) to explore the concept of queuing, then practise with Spider-Man and Lego® toys, and then go out into town to find opportunities to queue. Whether in the library or at the ice-cream van, the queues are shorter during the school day and the rewards more immediate. When I was confident that Sam had grasped the whole idea I would report back to school so that they were primed to observe and reward some 'good queuing' at school. Similar techniques worked for waiting, not interrupting, remembering to say please and thank you – a whole host of social skills that make the world an easier place.

As can be seen, the close working relationship with the school helped enormously with the success of these times. If Sam did something inappropriate at school, it could be reported to me. I had the time to get to the bottom of Sam's reason for doing or not doing whatever it was, and to work with him on a more acceptable alternative. I could then return this strategy to school, where they could use or reinforce it. Sam's world benefited from 'joined-up thinking'.

Of course, Sam's learning was not only about helping him with the social confusions caused by his autism. What is often not fully understood is to what extent autism can impact on academic learning. Sam, we know, has superior intelligence – but that didn't mean he was going to slip effortlessly into academic success. All sorts of things can stand in the way of success for the pupil with autism: social confusion, misunderstanding of language, sensory issues, fine motor skill problems, visual perception difficulties... the list is endless. Not all children with an ASD will have the same set of challenges, which makes it all the more difficult to put into place blanket supports for them in school. What flexischooling gave us was the opportunity to study Sam's specific difficulties and challenges, and to celebrate his specific strengths.

Although I am a teacher, I knew little or nothing about how this age group learned (I was more used to teaching Shakespeare to 18-year-olds!). Often when I discuss flexischooling as an option, parents will tell me that they lack the skills to teach their child. I don't believe this is the case. One of the advantages of flexischooling over full-time homeschooling is the huge amount of curriculum support that the educating parent can receive. You are not doing this on your own.

With Sam, we used the technique of bringing home worksheets, books and tasks from school. His teacher would give him these at each of his sessions in school and he would bring them home to complete. Through these we were able to see what he found incredibly easy (reading), what he was managing at about his age level (number work) and what he found difficult or impossible (writing). With each of these, this meant that we were able to work together to come up with academic tasks and supports wholly appropriate to Sam. With reading we concentrated on developing his understanding, particularly of characters and motivation. With number work we carried on with basic skills in line with his peers. And with writing…well, writing for us was a real issue.

It is not clear why so many children with an ASD struggle with handwriting (although several research projects are investigating) but, although not true for all, it does seem that this is an issue for a great many. Sam has an encyclopaedic memory, superior reasoning powers and an intelligent ability to order and connect what he knows… but he struggles to write even his own name. He cannot read what he 'writes', even for himself, and certainly no one else stands a chance. It remains a major frustration and a very real handicap to successful adult life, but at least we know his problems are not from lack of trying. We have done our best!

Sam's handwriting difficulty was obvious from very early, and immediately the school were able to offer various handwriting support courses. He took these at school and, of course, we had plenty of time to follow them up at home. Progress was pretty much non-existent. Next we tried physiotherapy. This was expensive and, since it took place during school time, would have been difficult to organise if Sam had been in school full time, but again we were able to give it our best shot. We tried Sensory Integration Therapy 1:1 programmes, but progress was extremely slow. We tried an at-home kinaesthetic approach, and continued with the programmes supplied by the school, but nothing seemed to make much difference.

Meanwhile, because he was at home so much, Sam was in a position to practise and develop his keyboard typing skills. Fortunately, handwriting is becoming less and less important in our modern world (it is a skill, Professor Attwood says, that is about as useful as being able to saddle a horse!). Sam is fluent on the computer. At school he was given a lightweight and robust word-processing keyboard to use. This was so successful that we bought our own, later upgrading it to a laptop computer as he grew up. Yes, I wish Sam could write as I can see how not being able to does let him down, but he hasn't let his inability stop him. Only some of the work we did through his education was ever about remediation, or 'putting right' missing skills. A great deal more was about accommodation, about finding ways for Sam to work round issues presented by his autism and still get the absolute best out of life. Flexischooling was excellent for this. Schools do offer remediation (although time and budget restrictions often mean that this is woefully little) but they are seldom placed to fully understand an individual's challenges and so support accommodation. Sam is the one who will live with autism all his life. He needs to know how to manage it, even enjoy it, and finding ways to do this has always seemed to us a very important part of his learning.

Our at-home time involved a considerable amount of formal, school-related work but there was always other time to be more flexible. One of the objections to flexischooling put forward by full-time home educators is that it is more restricted and less open to a more informal interpretation of what 'education' might involve. True, we always spent a good deal of time on traditional curriculum subjects and work set by the school, but there was always plenty of time left to us to be more inventive. Schools are slow places, as teachers try to manage the needs of 30 or so pupils at one time. Just getting from A to B takes time; setting up and packing up from lessons, queuing for lunch or snacks, waiting for others to get changed or catch up or settle down…so much of a pupil's time can just pass by. At home, with only one child to worry about, everything is so much quicker and we always seemed to have plenty of spare time left after academic work for other things.

Sam's 'extra' home time included everything from collecting and cataloguing mushrooms, visiting local castles and museums and trips to London, the theatre and science shows. It included planning and managing a trip by train from London to Sligo, visiting the land of the midnight sun in Norway, going to a David Attenborough lecture, training for and running a five-kilometre race, going strawberry picking, exploring cave art, making clay sculptures, writing a book and taking part in a DVD. There was always so much to do and most of it was tremendously enjoyable – for us both. Interaction with a child with an ASD is of paramount importance, and these times together gave us almost infinite opportunities to practise communication, without even realising we were doing it. Although part of Sam's education also included the need to practise everyday living skills – such as shopping, crossing roads, planning and budgeting – the very fact that he was in school for some of the time meant that we did not get too bogged down in these. I could get the family washing, shopping and cleaning done, largely, while he was in school, so that his at-home time was more fully focused on him and his needs. This always worked well for both of us, and I never felt torn between being a home teacher and being myself. I kept some protected time for myself to get jobs done, do freelance work and visit friends. Flexischooling may be less 'free' than full home education, but it is more structured and more supported and, as such, tends to be less intensive for all involved. Being with Sam is wonderful and has been one of the joys of my life...but even I needed a break sometimes!

Age 11–18

Meanwhile, Sam was growing up. The supportive and kindly world we had created between school and home had a time limit. Secondary school, high school (whatever you call it) provides an extremely challenging stage in the life of the person with an ASD. At age 11, it was time to 'move up'.

So often for the pupil with an ASD, this is when things start to fall apart. Quite often the younger pupils' environment can be made supportive enough for the pupil with an ASD to find a place for himself. Schools for younger pupils are usually smaller and each class tends to be taught by one main class teacher, who gets to know the pupils well. High schools are different. Now the school tends to be far larger, teachers are different for each subject, the day is confusing and demanding and each pupil is expected to manage in a far more independent way. In reality, for most neurotypical students this means relying on their peers. Which 'group' you fit into matters a great deal now, and how you manage the social demands of school can be just as important as how you manage the academic challenges.

Given all of this, it is perhaps surprising that flexischooling is generally less common for the older pupil than for the younger. Certainly we were told that it was most unlikely that it would be allowed to continue for Sam. It was 'an unheard of departure' for the school and it took considerable persuasion before we even got them to agree to consider it.

We kept on asking, thoroughly backed by Sam's current head teacher who was adamant that this system was working brilliantly for Sam. We also had the backing of our autism support specialists and paediatrician, and with all this support the school eventually agreed to a trial period. This was a very different atmosphere from the enthusiastic, team-shared approach we had enjoyed at Sam's primary school, but we crossed our fingers and hoped for the best. With luck, when they saw how well it worked, the staff at his new school would come round.

In fact, that isn't really what happened. Instead, what we managed to achieve was a kind of invisibility. This was a big school, very busy and very successful, with good academic attainment and high expectations of pupil behaviour. Where Sam would have run into difficulties would have been if his autism needs *hadn't* been being met. If he had got into the sort of chaos that was only too likely, if he had panicked or lashed out, run away or had a meltdown, then his autism would have been seen as an issue. As it was, he did none of these things. His only (potential) problem was that he was doing too well!

Because secondary schools have a timetable of individual subject lessons – each delivered by a different subject teacher – it appears to offer great challenges for flexischooling. In fact, it offers an ideal environment. Sam merely took rather fewer subjects than other pupils. For these subjects he was there full time, he did the same work as his peers, had the same homework and assignment expectations placed on him and underwent the same assessments. It was irrelevant to these subject teachers if, as he left their lessons, he was going on to a French class or going home. I'm not sure if all of his regular teachers were even fully aware of his flexischooling status.

The complication, of course, was with my time. If he had a day when he was in for registration and then history, out of school for a double lesson of geography, back for science and then out again for sport it did mean an awful lot of to-ing and fro-ing for me. On the other hand, this period of his life was relatively short. Within three or four years he had established himself enough, and grown up enough, to take himself to the library for independent study for some of his 'free' periods, and very soon after that he could get himself into and out of school, at least sometimes, independently on the bus. The investment of time spent on supporting him during his younger years, I am convinced, greatly helped his independence as he grew up.

What his individualised timetable gave him was the space to make the best of the time he was in school. Some years ago I shadowed a 15-year-old with a diagnosis of Asperger syndrome through his school days as part of study paper I was writing. I also got the chance to speak at length with his mother, and the experiences made a profound impression. The boy – I shall call him Mark – appeared to be managing school well. Certainly the school believed that he was an example of 'successful practice' for a child with an ASD. He was quiet and compliant in lessons and his work was usually done on time to a reasonable, if not exceptional, standard.

Shadowing him, though, I began to realise the tremendous strain he was under. One day, for example, he began with an English lesson, and was expected to work in a group discussing Thomas Hardy's use of metaphor. Mark could make no contribution whatsoever to this. Homework was set to write up what the group had discussed, which Mark probably didn't know. Immediately, without even a five-minute break, he was in physics and watching an experiment on sound waves. The class all grouped around the demonstration table and Mark, not liking crowds, held back, but not by so far as would be noticeable. I doubt he could see or hear a thing. Homework was set again – this time to write up the experiment, which of course he hadn't seen. After this he had a longish walk to his next class, which was history. The corridors were full and noisy and you had to physically push at times to make progress, particularly through the bottlenecks of the doors. This was supposed to be a break, but Mark spent it making his way to the next classroom and then allowing himself at least a few minutes' quiet when he arrived. Once the lesson started he got himself a corner seat to the far side of the classroom and seemed to 'zone out'. I doubt he followed any of the subsequent lesson, especially after the lights were dimmed in order to use a projected film on the whiteboard. And so his day went on.

Given how utterly overwhelming and confusing I found Mark's days to be, I was puzzled by how he was managing to keep up at all academically. The answer to this puzzle came when I talked to his mother. It turned out that she was doing most of it for him! She wasn't cheating, just trying her best to allow her son some chance of starting each day able to learn. She wrote up notes, copied and organised worksheets, worked out deadlines and timelines for assignments. She researched information he needed for essays so that he could be presented with clear, visually uncomplicated information from which to work. She acted as a scribe for him so that she typed as he spoke, speeding up what was otherwise the terribly slow and protracted business of trying to get his ideas down on paper.

Mark's mother told me that they would work together on trying to 'clear' his backlog from each day, from the time he got in from school until late into the evening, night after night. Often, she admitted, Mark would have to go up to bed, exhausted by the demands of the day, and she would finish the work by herself. She knew it couldn't go on, that she was neglecting her daughter, two years younger than Mark, and that her relationship with her husband was deteriorating. It was a nightmare-like situation but, as she said, what else could she do? There was no help available for a pupil as 'able' as Mark. If she didn't help him, she knew he would fail and she couldn't stand by and let that happen.

The difference between Mark's school experience and Sam's experience of flexischooling is time. We had time written into each day, because Sam had subjects he didn't take, when we could do all the copying up and scribing, the organising and collating, the researching and revising that Sam needed. Each typical school day came with an oasis of calm written into it, somewhere, when he could reflect and complete, comprehend and move on. It also came with time written into it for Sam to recharge, so that he re-entered the fray able to cope. Sam did not need to get to the point where Mark had been nearly all of the time: just about hanging on.

Because of his flexischooling, of course, Sam took rather fewer subjects in school than his peers. However, he was able to take all of the science subjects, which were his passion, and be in a position where he was able to achieve extremely well in them indeed. He was able to continue to read and research around these subjects so that his knowledge base was excellent. He also had the extra time to put in what was needed to achieve the necessary subjects he didn't enjoy so much and, additionally, the extra time to take some more 'off-beat' qualifications just out of interest. Some of these, indeed, are in autism and mean a greatly increased understanding of his own condition (although they tended to bring outrage at the negative perspective on the condition they can convey!). He has been able, in fact, to study all that he needed, and to study to the level he wanted.

Socially, Sam was happy – if a little peripheral – at school. He had a generally friendly attitude and never seemed to get into any unpleasantness, but he was rather like a visitor from another land: kindly disposed towards the natives but largely uncomprehending! On the other hand, his self-esteem remained high and he has always remained full of confidence in himself. Because of this, he has always been happy to join in any situation and has a wide range of friendly acquaintances of all ages. Genuine, close friendship is something else, but Sam has certainly never felt 'friendless'. Indeed, he has described himself as 'happy, clever and popular', which may be a better way of seeing oneself than many of us ever achieve!

The final great beauty of the flexischool model was how well it blended seamlessly into Sam's later life. By 18, all students at school had free study periods and all worked from home or in the library for large parts of their day. University students work this way too and many types of employment are either part time, flexible or can involve time working from home. The 'difference' that flexischooling can seem to bring simply fades away as the years pass.

As I said, the only potential problem Sam faced was that he did too well. Again and again, when staff realised that Sam attended school for only part of the time, they challenged that this was not necessary. It can be hard to see a polite, engaged, happy and confident pupil who is achieving at the top of his year group and who shows no signs of distress, and to understand why he needs to be part time at school. Since the only way to prove it would be to allow Sam to go back to full time, and so to risk failure, we never felt it was worth the danger just for the 'I told you so' factor. We cannot 'prove' that Sam is better off because of flexischooling, but we can trust our own judgement and – most important of all – we can trust Sam. We can believe him when he says that flexischooling has been best for him. With it, he has been able to *enjoy* school. He has not tolerated it, nor managed it, has not been 'getting by', 'just about coping' or 'doing okay with most of it', he has enjoyed it. I wonder how many people with autism are really able to say that.

Some Final Questions

Are there disadvantages to flexischooling?

Undoubtedly there are potential disadvantages – for the parents! By taking on flexischooling instead of allowing a school to take full-time responsibility for your child's education, you are accepting a huge commitment. Undoubtedly, your own professional development and economic security are likely to suffer. On the other hand, the wear and tear on you of sending your child off to school knowing that he is unhappy and underachieving, is itself incalculable. As an alternative to this, flexischooling is slightly less of a commitment than full-time homeschooling, and at least you get support, particularly academic support, from your child's contact with school. As I hope this book has shown, it is very unlikely that there will be disadvantages for your child. He will be getting an education far better tailored to both his academic needs and his ASD needs, and one that is entirely child centred. This will be an individual package and, as such, it works.

Can it work for the older child?

Absolutely. Often the older child with an ASD is more or less demanding this approach for himself. He may, to all intents and purposes, in his own mind have 'dropped' several subjects already, although the fallout, reprimands, detentions and so on that surround his decision not to do the work may still have to be borne. Formal flexischooling gives his needs more dignity and allows him to be a success – and to be socially polite and obliging rather than defiant.

What about working parents?

It is tough. Once you have you 'at-school' hours agreed for your child you are, of course, available for work yourself during those hours. Often though, particularly when your child is younger, school hours may be sporadic and unpredictable. Working at the school is perhaps one option, as is working from home (being a writer is ideal!). Generally, though, flexischooling does mean a commitment of your time and energy that is going to limit your own career and working development. It isn't for everyone, indeed not everyone is in a position to consider it, and unless you can persuade 'the powers that be' to recognise your huge contribution financially, that is not going to change. Good luck with that!

Doesn't he miss out on schoolwork?

As I have said, he is likely to be missing out on schoolwork anyway, through 'zoning out', not understanding, leaving the room or being sent out. Just how 'full time' full-time education actually is for most pupils with ASDs, is open to debate. When flexischooling works well it is an opportunity for a great deal more of the pupil's time to be spent learning productively. Yes, it may limit the number of subjects he can take initially, but it can help him to be successful at those subjects and encourage confidence in the business of learning so that his education can continue well into the future.

Can he still take exams?

In the UK the exams are independent and any pupil can be put in for them as an 'external' candidate (i.e. one not taught at that particular exam centre). The candidate may have to pay a registration fee, and it is important to get the paperwork for all of this sorted out well in advance. Other countries have different systems, but generally international barriers have fallen with the advent of the internet, and there is a far wider range of qualifications available to most people now than ever before.

How do you know what to teach?

As with the question above, the answer will depend on the exam. Each exam has a syllabus – the range of knowledge that will be tested in that qualification. As far as that goes, then, knowing what is needed is fairly simple. More difficult is knowing *how* to teach the skills and background learning needed, which is why flexischooling offers rather more support than going it alone through full-time homeschooling. Your child remains a pupil at the school and, as such, has access to the resources and expertise of that school, including any ASD expertise it may have.

Can he still have support in school?

Yes. He remains a member of that school and, as such, in the lessons he attends should be given the same support he would receive if he were there full time. Indeed, there is an argument that he should receive more since he is only there for some of the time and is therefore not using up the school's resources at other times. On the other hand, since flexischooling allows him to so much better meet his own needs, he may well need less support in the classroom anyway. Some of that 'support' will ideally now transfer to you and help build your expertise as his co-educator.

Do external agencies still give you support?

Any speech and language, paediatric or ASD-specific support you were getting already should still be available, since your child remains the 'patient'. Support that is normally given through school should also remain available to you, although you may have to ask for it. If flexischooling is working and your child is not being disruptive, aggressive or causing any disturbance, you may find that yours is not a priority case!

What do others who have tried flexischooling have to say?

At the moment there are no formal groups of people who have flexischooled with their children with an ASD. There are home educators who have tried flexischooling, and some of these do include parents whose children have ASD. These individual blogs and comments seem almost always to be positive: try searching for 'flexischooling' plus 'ASD' on an internet search engine for a selection. It may also be worth looking at Hollinsclough Primary school in Staffordshire, UK (www.hollinsclough.staffs.sch.uk/Flexi.htm) and Erpingham Primary school in Norfolk, UK (www.erpinghamprimaryschool.co.uk/smartweb/school/flexi-schooling). These schools are pioneering a new flexischooling approach available for all pupils, and offer an interesting wider perspective.

I don't have the expertise to teach him! Can we still flexischool?

Again, the answer may be to work with the school. The school has the expertise to teach; you have (or will develop) the expertise in your individual child. Remember, the aim is to allow your child to grow to a point where he is in charge of his own learning, and his own ASD. Ultimately, it is his expertise rather than that of home or school that matters, and home and school working together in partnership with him is the most likely combination to lead to eventual success.

Don't siblings feel hard done by?

Undoubtedly, many siblings are going to feel that this system is a bit unfair. On the other hand, one of the advantages of flexischooling is that you are not so overwhelmed by the needs of your child with an ASD during the rest of the time. By having dedicated 1:1 time with your more 'needy' child, you are free to give his neurotypical siblings the normal levels of attention, homework nagging, 'Why don't you tidy your room?' attention as you normally would! Take time to explain to your other children and help them to understand. In spite of sibling rivalry, most will be hurt by their brother or sister's unhappiness in school and will almost certainly be anxious about your levels of distress if his or her needs are not being met. If flexischooling means that everything is calmer, there should be rewards for everyone – your neuro-typical children included.

Isn't it an organisational nightmare for my disorganised child?

Organisational difficulties are often some of the unseen problem producers of the child with an ASD. 'Impaired executive functioning', as it is more grandly called, often leads to an apparent bubble of chaos surrounding the child – with books and papers crumpled, notes not handed in, homework lost or not completed and completed assignments mislaid. The result is that the child appears 'careless' and will often be in trouble for this, leading to further loss of confidence and self-esteem. Flexischooling gives islands of calm in each day when work can be collected, completed, ordered and properly presented. You may find that each Tuesday afternoon slot is entirely given over to helping your child make sense of, complete and copy up the work done on Tuesday morning, but at least that work does get done and your child is able to make progress. It is very hard to learn when all is in disarray. More importantly, it is hard for the child to learn to manage chaos and create order unless he has regular opportunities to take stock and catch up. The end target is an adult who manages to be organised, and who is relaxed enough about it that he doesn't need to sink into obsession. This is a real and valid learning objective for a pupil with an ASD, so never feel defensive about the many hours you dedicate to it.

My relationship with the school is already rather tense. Will we be able to work together?

That depends on how far things have gone, and how ready either side is to start again. Perhaps it would help if your child were moved sideways to a new class or to a different set of teachers, so that you can all 'start again'. If you feel this isn't enough, you could always sound out alternative schools. Starting afresh at a school that is willing to embrace the philosophy of flexischooling for pupils with an ASD is often an easier option.

My school says flexischooling is illegal. What can I do?

In the kindest possible way, educate the staff involved! Flexischooling is a legal option as long as the child's education is both full time and 'appropriate'. Arm yourself with the facts, and take the time to familiarise yourself with their arguments against flexischooling, most of which are likely to be unfounded concerns about position and resources. If what you are doing is for the best of your child – and it can help to get your paediatrician or education psychologist on board here – they really should not be able to put up any viable barriers. A flexischooling request is a valid request and should be considered on its own merits. What is more, it should not be rejected unless the school can come up with valid and tangible reasons for it to be refused.

What if he still hates the parts of school he does go in for?

Although flexischooling can calm the school 'issue' down for the pupil with an ASD, there may well still be much about school that he finds difficult, particularly if his previous experience has been negative. Work with the school and see if together you can find ways of helping your child to manage the environment. Perhaps you could reduce his in-school time still further until you come to a point where he is genuinely happy. This can be built on and together you, the school and your child can find ways to make school a success. Keep talking to your child and to the school, and make sure that everyone holds on to the priority of making this work. Although full-time home education is always an option, this should always be a positive choice and should never come about just because you have given up. Flexischooling can make school work, so keep on trying!

Whose responsibility is it to make sure he is getting a 'full-time education'?

In England, this responsibility is always with the parent, so if your child is not receiving a 'full-time' education at school when attending full time, for the reasons discussed, technically it is your responsibility! With flexischooling you may well have to demonstrate how your child is getting a full-time education during his home-education time, although it is unlikely that you will have to do so for his in-school time. Ideally, you and the school will work together to ensure that his learning is seamless and constant, for everybody's good.

Does it work?

Flexischooling is only one way forward for the successful education of the child with an ASD, and it is not for everyone. It may always remain a rather minority approach, one that not everyone chooses to try and not all those who do try choose to use longer term. It is, though, an option that does work for many children with an ASD. It makes their school days far more successful and enjoyable and removes the fear, stress and unhappiness that full-time school means for so many of these children. Flexischooling can allow parents to be fully involved and for school professionals to work with parents for the good of the pupil. It allows the child with an ASD to grow into the adult with an ASD with understanding and even appreciation of his condition, and with strategies in place to remain successful into adult life. Yes, I believe that flexischooling for the child with an ASD does work. I hope this book has helped in your decision as to whether to give it a try yourself. Good luck!

Into the Future

Flexischooling, I believe, can work wonderfully as an educational support for the child with an ASD. It combines genuine flexibility, a completely individual, child-centred approach, full opportunity for parental expertise and involvement, and a respectful and sensitive appreciation of the needs of a child with an ASD into the current, already available, model of education.

But is it fair? Parents are desperate to do what is best for their children and may be willing to give up their own careers and aspirations, to vastly reduce their incomes and to work in isolation, often facing suspicion and ridicule, in order to do what they can to help make their child's life better. Is it fair to expect them to do this and in this way to take on this lion's share of responsibility for their child's learning and development?

I think the answer to this pivots on the word 'expect'. This book is passionate about giving parents the *opportunity* for this level of involvement, about making sure that parents are aware that they *should be allowed* to be involved like this and about giving flexischooling to parents as *another option*. What it is not doing is suggesting that this is what all parents should be 'expected' to do, particularly in a climate where they are, in fact, expected to be grateful for the opportunity! There is something very odd about a system where this is what we have to argue.

I believe, along with experts such as Mary Warnock and Lorna Wing to name but two, that something has to be done about the current education opportunities for our children with an ASD. The situation, as it stands, is simply not good enough and is not meeting the needs of all our children in a way that is even close to acceptable. As Mary Warnock says: 'However tolerant and supportive the policies and however understanding the members of staff, there are limits to what realistically can be achieved in mainstream schools, given the diversity of children's needs and the finite resources available' (Warnock in Cigman, 2007). Nor is the price of failure something to ignore: 'The tragic result for some children with autistic difficulties is trauma and even regression' (*ibid*).

Flexischooling does work, but sadly it is never going to be an answer available to very many unless it is recognised and formalised, unless the huge contribution that parents are able (and willing) to offer through it is recognised and supported, both financially and socially. The resource that these parents offer is one that, I believe, is desperately in need of recognition. If society could do this, and could support their contribution seriously, through financial recognition and social respect, the benefits would be immense. After all, Inclusion is not really about where children are educated, but about how. 'Inclusion', as Ruth Cigman puts it, 'is a "process" rather than an environment'. Surely, if we can all, as in Meighan's (1988) definition of flexischooling, share responsibility for our children's education in agreed contract and partnership, then that process stands a much better chance of success.

References and Further Reading

References

Attwood, T. (2005) In The National Autistic Society 'Bullying: A guide for parents'. Available at www.autism.org.uk/living-with-autism/education/primary-and-secondary-school/your-child-at-school/bullying-a-guide-for-parents.aspx, accessed on 12 March 2012.

Attwood, T. (2007) *The Complete Guide to Asperger's Syndrome*. London: Jessica Kingsley Publishers.

Badman, G. (2009) *Report to the Secretary of State on the Review of Elective Home Education in England*. London: The Stationery Office.

Batten, A., Corbett, C., Rosenblatt, M., Withers L. and Yuille, R. (2006) *Make School Make Sense: Autism and Education: The Reality for Families Today*. London: The National Autistic Society.

Cigman, R. (ed.) (2007) *Included or Excluded*. London: Routledge.

Hesmondhalgh, M and Breakey, C. (2001) *Access and Inclusion for Children with Autistic Spectrum Disorders*. London: Jessica Kingsley Publishers.

Lawrence, C. (2008) *How to Make School Make Sense*. London: Jessica Kingsley Publishers.

Madders, T. (2010) *You Need to Know*. London: The National Autistic Society.

Meighan, R. (1988) *Flexi-schooling*. Ticknall: Education Now.

Oliver, K. (2000) 'Felxi-time Schooling: Towards Flexi-Schooling and felxi-education.' Available at http://flexitimeschooling.org/fts.pdf, accessed on 8 May 2012.

Rosenblatt, M. (2008) *I Exist: The Message from Adults with Autism in England*. London: The National Autistic Society.

Wing, L and Gould, J. (1979) 'Severe impairments of social interaction and associated abnormalities in children: Epidemiology and classification.' *Journal of Autism and Developmental Disorders 9*, 11–29.

Further reading

Attwood, T. (2007) *The Complete Guide to Asperger's Syndrome*. London: Jessica Kingsley Publishers.

Consultation on Elective Home Education Guidelines. Available at www.education. gov.uk/consultations/downloadableDocs/Elective%20Home%20 Education%20Guidelines%201.doc, accessed on 12 April 2012.

Deutsch, D. and Wolf, K. (1991) *Home Education and the Law* (2nd edition). Oxford: Deutsch and Wolf.

Dowty, T. and Cowlishaw, K. (2002) *Home Educating our Autistic Spectrum Children – Paths are Made by Walking*. London: Jessica Kingsley Publishers.

Fortune-Wood, M. *Flexi School*. Available at www.home-education.org.uk/ articles/article-flexi-school.pdf, accessed on 12 March 2012.

Gutherson, P. and Mountford-Lees, J. (2010) *New Models for Organising Education: 'Flexi-schooling' – How One School Does it Well*. Reading: CfBT Education Trust.

Hampshire County Council (2008) *Home Education* FAQ. Available at www3. hants.gov.uk/education/parents-info/home-education/home-education-faq.htm, accessed on 12 March 2012.

Lawrence, C. (2007) *Finding Asperger Syndrome in the Family: A Book of Answers*. Brighton and Hove: Emerald.

Lawrence, C. (2010) *Explaining Autism Spectrum Disorder*. Brighton and Hove: Emerald.

Lawrence, C. (2010) *Successful School Change and Transition for the Child with Asperger Syndrome: A Guide for Parents*. London: Jessica Kingsley Publishers.

Leicestershire County Council (2008) *Flexischooling: Guidance for Schools*. Available at www.leics.gov.uk/lcc_flexischooling_guidance.pdf, accessed on 12 March 2012.

Meighan, R. *Flexi-schooling, Year-round Education (YRE) and Cyber Schools*. Available at www.rolandmeighan.co.uk/resources/Flexischooling.pdf, accessed on 12 March 2012.

Schetter, P. and Lighthall, K. (2009) *Homeschooling the Child with Autism*. San Francisco: Jossey Bass/Wiley.

Winter, M. (2011) *Asperger Syndrome – What Teachers Need to Know: Second Edition*. London: Jessica Kingsley Publishers.

Index